Praise for Conscious Fo

MW01119928

Reading Dianne Eppler Ac personally stimulating, wisdom-packed and transforming massage for your heart and brain. Dianne offers us not only her personal insights, gleaned from decades of her own compelling life experiences, but shares with us her warm heart, her personal depth and her remarkable visionary gifts. Each chapter of this innovative book is like attending a soul-inspiring event – a true treasure for those whose consciousness is expansive, open and curious. As you allow Dianne to guide you through insight-filled reflections on self-awareness, personal empowerment, conscious relationship, purposeful creation and expansive vision, you find yourself magically expanded, softly deepened and intimately transformed. Dianne's heart-full sharing, her engaging writing style, and her deep honesty are potent trademarks of a book well worth your reading. In recommending this exciting book to you, I suggest that you use it daily as an ongoing guide for self-expansion.

~ Bill Bauman, author,
Soul Vision: a Modern Mystic Looks at Life through the Eyes of the Soul

Dianne Adams has written an inspiring yet practical guide for daily living and for connecting to your own inner wisdom. She offers honest and authentic reflections to help you find happiness by recognizing Spirit in the ordinary activities of life. Posing deep questions gleaned from her own life experiences, Dianne will powerfully inspire, encourage and challenge you to find purpose and meaning in your life.

~ Corinne McLaughlin, co-author,
The Practical Visionary and *Spiritual Politics*

Dianne Eppler Adams shows us how to bring spiritual consciousness into everyday life. *Conscious Footsteps* provides insight and perspective for the contemporary spiritual journey. As far away as we think we may be from connection to a higher power, there is no place, no event in our lives, in which wisdom and guidance are not present. *Conscious Footsteps* will touch your heart and guide your soul!

~ Gisele Terry, M.A., CAP, President,
International Society for Astrological Research

Conscious Footsteps

Finding Spirit in Everyday Matters

⤐⤏

By Dianne Eppler Adams

Jacqueline!
Your friendship has
inspired my conscious
growth since the moment
we met. Thank you, Dear One!

author·HOUSE®

AuthorHouse™
1663 Liberty Drive
Bloomington, IN 47403
www.authorhouse.com
Phone: 1-800-839-8640

© *2010 Dianne Eppler Adams. All rights reserved.*

No part of this book may be reproduced, stored in a retrieval system, or transmitted by any means without the written permission of the author.

First published by AuthorHouse 6/3/2010

ISBN: 978-1-4520-1149-3 (e)
ISBN: 978-1-4520-1147-9 (sc)

Library of Congress Control Number: 2010905787

Printed in the United States of America
Bloomington, Indiana

This book is printed on acid-free paper.

To my mother, Dorothy, for instilling early the joy of words by reading me fairy tales; my father, Grant, for proving to me that what you set your mind to do you can achieve; my beloved husband, Chuck, for teaching me unconditional love every day; and my daughters, Erica and Erin, for being kindhearted and caring beings.

Acknowledgments

It is impossible to include all the people who have helped make this book a reality. Those who have encouraged, taught, supported, and urged me forward measure in the hundreds. As sure as the Sun rises, I have forgotten someone, but here are the most significant people:

For encouragement to write ~ Marita Golden, Jill Lublin, and my many newsletter readers

For expert editing assistance ~ Joanne Shwed of Backspace Ink, Juanita Ruth One, and Mary Kay Paulson

For soulfully photographing the author – Elizabeth of ElizabethLinares. com

For personal support and encouragement ~ Loretta Proctor, Jacqueline Janes, Lori Rock, Bev Hitchins, and my dear sisters-in-law, Peg Adams and Pat Aldridge

For spiritual mentoring ~ Bill and Donna Bauman, Gordon Davidson and Corinne McLaughlin, and Gerry Judd

For deepening my social consciousness ~ Danaan Perry, Margaret Wheatley, and Sharif Abdullah

For guidance and support on my life's journey, I acknowledge my inner guidance. Consciously and unconsciously, I am blessed with support from the unseen world every moment of my life. For that, I am eternally grateful.

Table of Contents

In the Beginning

In 2004, I launched my monthly New Moon newsletter, *Spirit in Matters*, from which much of the material in this book has been drawn. At the time, it felt risky to think that anyone would be interested in my ideas but, despite my caution, one day I found myself writing this:

> A time has come for me, when the inner urge is too great to ignore. When looking out at the world, its events, and people, there seems to be a better way. Or at least I seek to ask the questions that would open up an image or discussion of a better way to find personal fulfillment while living on the earth together, managing our differences, and learning how to grow into a truly global community. This is not a remote intellectual exercise, but a deep, heartfelt search for new possibilities.
>
> The first step of the journey, I believe, begins with an honest and truthful view of things just as they are. Radical honesty is called for, without illusion. I do not propose to have complete answers to the issues I raise. For every issue, there may be two or probably more possible points of view. By carrying on a discussion of the issues closest to my heart, I hope to encourage a thoughtful search for a better, more harmonious, more loving way to evolve.

As in my newsletter, I write this book with a particular point of view. The following beliefs continue to guide my inquiry:

+ We live in an interconnected universe. A butterfly flapping its wings in Argentina has an effect on the winds in Siberia. Some call it "the Oneness Principle." I seek to recognize and honor the interdependence and sacredness of all life.
+ All relationships—personal, communal, national, global, as well

as plant, animal, and mineral—are of equal worth. We are at our best when we approach them with the values of fairness, respect, honesty, and compassion.

◆ Darkness in the human experience is overcome not through avoidance or only looking at "the sweetness of life" but through shining the light of awareness on the darkness and choosing otherwise.

By sharing my journey and my beliefs in this book, I invite you to take "conscious footsteps" forward toward your own personal wholeness and abundant living.

~ Dianne Eppler Adams

Introduction

We do not receive wisdom; we must discover it for ourselves,
after a journey through the wilderness
which no one else can make for us, which no one can spare us.
For our wisdom is the point of view
from which we come at last to regard the world.

~ Marcel Proust

As you begin reading, you will realize that this is not a "how-to" book, giving you steps and procedures to arrive at a desired destination. It is a "what if?" book meant to trigger your own awareness and inner guidance.

I offer my observations—the thoughts of a "practical mystic" who seeks to integrate her understanding of Spirit as it manifests in the midst of ordinary life. My observations are intended to raise questions for you.

By raising questions, I intend to move toward answers, but as Rilke reminds us in the following verse, we need patience to "live the questions" in hope of some day finding answers:

> Be patient toward all that is unsolved in your heart and try to love the questions themselves like locked rooms and like books that are written in a foreign tongue. Do not now seek the answers, which cannot be given you because you would not be able to live them. And the point is, to live everything. Live the questions now. Perhaps you will find them gradually, without noticing it, and live along some distant day into the answer.
>
> ~ Rainer Maria Rilke

As you read, you will note the key questions explored in this book:

- What if Spirit is present in every facet of my existence? What if Spirit is working through the guy who cut me off in traffic in the same way that Spirit works through the guy ahead of me in the toll booth who surprisingly paid my toll?
- How would my life be different if I knew that everyone and everything was a part of me?
- Who would I be and how would I behave if I recognized that there is no separation between me and God – never was – and that I am not only created by God but I am part of God?

For millennia, those who walked the conscious path of spiritual development chose to leave the world and retire to a cave to meditate and evolve. Today, many spiritual seekers find that their spiritual path has become divorced from a religious setting. So many seekers describe themselves as "spiritual but not religious" that it can be considered a separate religious denomination.

Clearly, the contemporary spiritual journey is taking many pilgrims to the "cave of the heart" and then outward into the world. Thomas Moore, author of *Care of the Soul*, affirms that "you don't find Spirit by moving away from the mundane; you find it by going more generously into the ordinary."

To illustrate, my former mentor, Danaan Perry, used to speak of "Parvati's Fire" from the Vedas of India. Parvati's Fire is described as the holy fire that burns away our personas and veils of illusion so that we can access our spiritual core. He would say, "If you want to stand close to Parvati's Fire, you must do two things: get involved in a relationship and go to the marketplace." Our relationships and our interactions in the workplace provide more than enough opportunities to evolve.

As a contemporary spiritual pilgrim, I have been blessed to witness and explore a myriad of life's possibilities. Always seeking greater awareness, it is with great joy that I share my insights, which I view as gifts from the Divine, as they move through me.

Many of my insights are drawn from the fact that I am a professional astrologer. Astrology has been a marvelous tool to open my consciousness to a greater reality. However, you do not need to believe in, understand, or care about astrology to benefit from reading this book. For those who would like to know a bit more about astrology, the appendix will provide some basic information.

If my insights have meaning for you, it is because you are feeling a resonance with the truth of your own connection to the Divine. Cherish yourself as a unique and miraculous aspect of the Divine in human form. We are all part of the Divine. Unfortunately, not everyone is spiritually aware, but you would not have picked up this book if you were not seeking deeper awareness.

I encourage you to open this book to any page at any time. Use it to inspire your day in the morning or to trigger restful sleep at night. May it offer you hope in the midst of turmoil and be a tool to awaken your own inner wisdom—the best and truest guidance you will ever find.

You are beginning your journey of opening to Spirit in the matters of your everyday life!

ॐ◌ॐ

The inner can only fully reveal its meaning when it is lived in everyday life. The outer world gives it color and substance, makes it real. And only when something becomes real can we understand its true purpose: what it means to us. The combination of the inner and the outer brings alive the secrets of life.

~ Llewellyn Vaughan-Lee

Chapter 1

Cultivating Awareness of Spirit

The Divine is not something high above us.
It is in heaven, it is in earth, it is inside us ...
It is right here in this very body.
Each one of us is a miniature universe, a living shrine.

~ Morihei Ueshiba

What is Spirit?

If we look at the path, we do not see the sky. We are earth people on a spiritual journey to the stars. Our quest, our earth walk, is to look within, to know who we are, to see that we are connected to all things, that there is no separation, only in the mind.

~ Native American, source unknown

ॐॐ

There is an essence that can be found in everything that exists. It is interwoven in the fabric of all life—in a grain of sand, in a ripe apple, in a sleeping cat, in a balmy breeze, and in you and me. It is the tie that binds everything in physical existence and in the unseen realm.

I call this connecting force Spirit. You may know it as Soul, God, Goddess, the Divine, Creator, or whatever other name speaks to you.

Like the wind or electricity, it cannot be seen, yet it can indeed be known and experienced. Even if you are not aware of Spirit, it is nevertheless ever-present and ever-pervasive in all that exists.

The absence of the awareness of Spirit is the cause of great suffering, conflict, and despair. Without conscious awareness of Spirit, we are separated from our Self—our true identity—which is eternal and unchanging. We are also separated from, and in conflict one way or another with, everyone and everything around us.

When we open to finding Spirit in everyday matters, we are healing the ultimate cause of all suffering, and restoring the true harmony and peace that is who we really are.

Thinking that we are separate individuals or that we are somehow more important than the flowers, the birds, or the mountains dooms us to struggle as victims of the past or hope we can be powerful in the future. All the while, the key to lasting peace is hidden within this very moment (yes, the one you are reading in right now!).

Awareness of Spirit's presence in the moment heals our sense of separation and opens up the universe as our home. Only the ego could be crazy enough to seek the puny goal of power and influence for itself alone, when there is no limit to what is possible when you are aware of Spirit.

Well, then, what are we waiting for? Our wholeness and consciousness of Oneness with all life is merely a present moment away.

Come Home to the Moment

People look in vain places for peace. They seek it in the world outside, in places, people, ways, activities . . . but there is no peace found this way. They are looking in the wrong direction, and the longer they look the less they find what they are looking for.

~ Meister Eckhart

❧❧

Eckhart's words came to me from an inner voice at an uncomfortable moment during a long trip. I was feeling discombobulated by the travel, moving to a new campsite every night, and never knowing whether we'd have cell phone coverage or an ability to read email.

I felt disoriented by having all my normal routines disrupted and it felt pretty uncomfortable. On the other hand, a change of routine was the very thing I had been looking forward to. It brings to mind the adage, "Be careful what you wish for; you might get it."

I think my inner voice was trying to teach me that there is the opportunity to know "home" in every moment of our lives. A sense of home is very important for me. It is a place of safety and security to be myself. As much as I love to roam, my nesting instinct is very strong. To survive, I made our tent camper my nest.

On a much deeper level, however, we all carry within us a sense of home that comes from our Soul's connection to Spirit. Our connection to Spirit is eternal and provides our true security, that which our physical home only represents.

I am learning that whatever is happening in the moment to distress me—like torrential rain when the bathroom is far from my campsite, or needing to make a call when there's no cell coverage—is a fleeting issue. If I spend my time focused on the discomfort or injustice, or whatever thought I use to resist the moment, I am disconnecting from my true sense of home. That sense of home is something I carry with me in every moment.

Learning to come home to the moment comes by opening our awareness to the Divine. That is a choice we can make in every moment of our lives.

Strength from Beyond

The presence of fear is a sure sign you are trusting in your strength.

~ *A Course in Miracles*

❧ ❦

I recently came across this quote and it brought a chuckle to my heart. It never hurts to be reminded that, when we become paralyzed with fear of something that has come up, we may be erroneously thinking that our strength is the only way to deal with it. However, we don't have to do it alone. We have hidden support from Spirit as well as others who may appear to offer us help.

Being independent, I am prone to taking initiative and shouldering responsibilities for whatever comes my way. How about you? Are you likely to be a solo performer when you could ask for help? Most tasks are easier and get finished faster when others help.

However, there is another form of support and strength I suggest we need to remember. It supports all of us, all of the time, and it's unseen. You may call it whatever you'd like. I call it Spirit and consider its actions a mystery. Spirit's assistance may appear as a flash of insight, a whisper on the wind, a vision in the clouds, or a stroke of what some would call "good luck."

I remind myself that I did not create myself. Therefore, I am not the beginning and end of the strength on which I can call to manage my life. I frequently call on Spirit during the day with an inner thought or wish or prayer. I ask for strength when I feel weak. I ask for clarity when I am confused. I ask for patience when I am frustrated.

The operation of Spirit is not something I fully understand, but I trust it. I consider it humorous that, with our little brains, we think we might understand the vast wisdom of Spirit. For this reason, I believe all religions and belief systems are only partially true. All mystics, seers, and prophets see part of the Truth but not the Whole Truth. They are trying to access the Truth with a puny (relatively speaking) instrument called "the human mind."

When I am fearful, I call on the strength that comes from beyond me and trust that Spirit is handling everything.

Primary Networking ~ Go Within

Do not give yourself entirely to activity and do not engage in active works all the time. Keep something of your heart and of your time for meditation.

~ Bernard de Clairvaux

❧⟩⟨❧

I keep myself so busy every day that I often find it hard to sit down and meditate. Now, I am sure I am not the only one who has that trouble, right? During a certain period, I had been particularly busy, going to local business networking groups including my own Holistic Entrepreneurs Alliance. When I finally sat down, got quiet, and listened, what I heard made me produce an audible laugh. "You know," I chucked to myself, "all that networking you've been doing? You need to get your priorities straight and remember your primary network—within your Self."

It is very easy to get too focused on making connections with others, thinking that they hold the answer to making our lives work. Attention on business relationships and promotion of our services to others may appear to be what leads to success. However, if we aren't in tune with our Inner Self, what exactly are we offering?

It is only by going within—doing our "primary networking"—that we remain aware of who we really are and what our mission is. Without constant clarity gained from our own inner voice or Higher Self, it is quite easy to get off course, spin our wheels, and get nowhere fast.

When I remember to meditate, life is more effortless, answers arise when I need them, and I don't get pulled off track either by trying to please another or by acting out of alignment with my Higher Self.

Here's an example: During one of those times when I was so busy doing outer activities that I forgot to go within, I hastily offered help to someone. Unfortunately, by doing this, I would have detoured away from my own intended path. Fortunately, she understood when I called back and explained my inability to carry through with my offer.

Had I just stopped and gone within before impulsively offering, I would have realized the right course of action. Sometimes it pays to respond slowly and to first seek Soul's guidance.

Before you make major decisions or take bold actions, remember your "primary networking" and go within your Self. Then, when you do act, you are more likely to be acting authentically from your Higher Self or Soul's guidance.

Living from the Inside Out

What lies behind us and what lies before us are tiny matters compared to what lies within us.

~ Ralph Waldo Emerson

❧ ☙

During a recent trip to India, I became aware of the importance of getting my priorities straight. It is not the world that gives us life but the inner spark of the Divine that lives through us and animates us. Why then do I go to the computer to answer my email the first thing in the morning? My mind gets caught up with outer stuff—worries, concerns, and hopes— before I connect to my Divine Source.

The daily rituals in a Hindu's life can be quite mundane and yet they are done with great reverence and devotion, highlighting the Sacred in everyday activities. Standing on the banks of the Ganges River at dawn, I observed a simple bathing ritual that surely originated from the beginning of time. This was not just a body cleansing ritual; it was purification with sacred devotion to the Divine Source of all life.

Living from the inside out makes me conscious of my inner peace, no matter what is happening around me. I maintain greater awareness and thus find guidance for taking wise actions in every moment.

How do I know this? While I was on my India journey, I was able to maintain my inner awareness, which lasted for a couple weeks afterward.

Yet, after two or three days of feeling frustrated that I had not gotten much done, I realized I was back in the old rut of piling too much on my "to-do" list and then plowing forward haphazardly, seeking to cross off the highest number of items. Priorities were not necessarily considered and I was sidetracked by many little distractions. In fact, I was once again putting email ahead of my meditation and journaling time.

When I start my day with meditation and journaling, I begin with a reminder that all the energy and answers I need for my life lie within me. Then I am more likely to carry that awareness into the activities of my day. Conversely, when I start with email, I get drawn into fighting fires or simply reacting to outer stimuli, like a floating leaf dashed about in a raging stream.

Our current times are chaotic when we focus on the changing tides outside. We will all do well to remember that our good does not come from any outer source. Our good comes from our relationship to our Higher Self within us. Consider placing the highest priority on your inner world, so you can face whatever the outer world presents with greater confidence and peace.

Interpreting Reflections

What you are searching for is what is searching.

~ St. Francis of Assisi

આ⸱૯

As I have grown to understand how life works, one particular skill has served me well. It is a learned skill, not one that comes naturally, which I call "interpreting reflections."

Opposite our interior world or inner feelings is our external world or our awareness of what is happening outside and around us. The people and happenings and the circumstances of our daily life are continually providing us with information. We constantly act and react with the external world, but how often do we consider the meaning and significance of what we see or what is happening?

I believe there is much to gain from interpreting the reflections we receive from the external world. In other words, look at the significance of the behavior of others toward you. Consider whether they might be sending a subtle message, not overtly said but implied. If I am emotionally triggered by their behavior, could it be that they are mirroring a behavior of my own that I don't like? The good or bad we see in another is quite likely present in us. We may have disowned those qualities and projected them on others.

If that is true, then, when we look outward, I believe we can get a hint of what is happening inside ourselves. In fact, one way your unconscious or subconscious speaks to you is through the people and circumstances you experience moment by moment.

How does this work?

When I worked for a nonprofit organization, my relationships with my co-workers were abysmal. I loved the work I was doing and believed in the purpose of the organization, but I kept running into snags with others in the office. I even experienced my boss as disempowering when he told me I was a poor writer. Believing him, the only writing I did for several years after that was in my personal journal.

While at that job, I figured that I just worked with a bunch of jerks. If I had been open to *interpreting reflections*, I would have realized what I know now. My writing was poor because the subject matter (technical project reports) was uninteresting to me. My interpersonal relations were terrible because my own self-criticism and self-doubt threw me out of balance with my Inner Self. I was working in a technical environment with a "get-it-done-at-all-costs" mentality, disregarding the yearning of my heart to relate to others on a deeper, more spiritual basis.

If I had interpreted reflections then, I would have left gracefully after finding more appropriate work. Instead, I quit in a huff and ended up unemployed for several months. Oh, what a lesson I learned!

This past week, I had the opportunity to share this perspective with a client. I pointed out that the reason the foundations of her life were falling apart was that her life no longer fit who she was becoming. Her seeming life breakdown was actually evidence of inner growth.

How did I know? I knew because I could interpret the reflections she was getting from the outer world as evidence of the beginning of a whole new sense of herself. Although unknown, the future will present her with a life that more naturally fits her newly aware Self.

Interpreting reflections has many other uses. Have you ever wondered why some days everyone is angry around you? At a time like this, check inside to see if you have any simmering feelings of frustration or rage. Have you been holding yourself back from action due to self-doubt?

I am not suggesting that all people's actions around you are directly tied to you. I am suggesting that when something happens more than once, or it affects you very intensely, it might be something personally meaningful. It is worth taking the time to interpret the reflection with a willingness to make a course correction based on your new awareness.

I remember reading about a Buddhist monk who, every day, looking out at all the troubles of the world, resolved to take action by looking inside himself to find such things as conflict, greed, and deception, and heal himself. That is truly where world peace begins.

May you find great benefit from interpreting the reflections from your external world.

Aquarian Wisdom on a Coffee Cup

People need to see that, far from being an obstacle, the world's diversity of languages, religions and traditions is a great treasure, affording us precious opportunities to recognize ourselves in others.

~ Youssou N'Dour, musician

෩ ෨

When we open up to living with Spirit in our everyday lives, it seems that Spirit's wisdom is all around us.

After a very long, exhausting plane trip from the Far East, the first thing I did was race for the Starbucks' stand to get my favorite drink—a decaf Americano. Swilling down the lovely brew, I noticed Youssou N'Dour's quote on the side of the cup.

My heart swelled with joy as I read the description of my journey for the past few months. Blessed to have spent a month in India and then two weeks in Thailand and Cambodia, I mostly enjoyed the opportunities to find myself in the many faces and various faiths of those whom I met.

The theme of finding "unity in diversity," if really implemented in our world, would allow each of us to shine in our own uniqueness. We would have no need to measure ourselves against anyone else because our differences would be appreciated and we would never have to feel rejected or alone. Contributing our unique gifts, while still being able to ask when we have a need others can provide, would bring more harmony into our daily living.

We are moving ever closer as a society to when this approach will become even more important. To thrive in a time of economic challenge, we will need to draw around us a tighter community for mutual benefit and support.

As we move into the Age of Aquarius, the old Piscean devotion to hierarchical power is falling away, while the value of "equality and fraternity" between people is gaining emphasis. Since the founding of the United States, the world has been moving in that direction toward a more humane and equalitarian society.

Reminders of our mutual interests are everywhere—even on a Starbucks' coffee cup!

God Has No Religion, Race, or Gender

Do not think of knocking out another person's brains because he differs in opinion from you. It would be as rational to knock yourself on the head because you differ from yourself ten years ago.

~ Horace Mann

❧

Naturally, everyone has an opinion about God. Even atheists hold a point of view, albeit one that finds God nonexistent. You probably reached your opinion through parental influence, church involvement, or perhaps through reading scriptures or spiritual books. However, of one thing I am certain: It is not the whole picture or the Whole Truth about God. No one knows the complete Truth.

Since we are each an aspect of Creation, how can we possibly know about the Whole of which we are a part? We have only our individual point of view with which to look at Creation. From such a limited vantage point, are we not arrogant to assume that we know God, what God is, and what God wants from us?

Major wars have been and continue to be caused by differing views of God and perceptions of God's rules for living. While some religions are tolerant of differences, many belief systems hold that their view of God is the "one and only way to salvation."

If all Creation has emanated from God, just one religion, race, or gender cannot be said to be the "one way." God includes all religions, all races, and all genders.

So what does this realization mean for me in my everyday life? I am separating myself from God, from my own Source, whenever I act as if my way is the only "right" way; whenever I view my religion as "the only true religion"; whenever I criticize and separate myself from other people, cultures, and religions. My thoughts of separation harm me as they shut down my openness to the wonder and blessings streaming to me from God in every moment, in every situation.

God has no religion, race, or gender. God includes all religions, races, and genders—even you and me.

What Does it Mean to "Thrive"?

When you realize there is nothing lacking, the whole world belongs to you.

~ Lao-tzu

৵৹ৼ

The word "thrive" is defined as "to grow, flourish, and prosper." To me, the idea of thriving is the experience of being aware and alive, ever-growing and expanding my sense of my Self, who I am, and why I am here—my purpose.

This feeling of thriving can exist in the midst of difficulty. When challenges are great, you can still grow in conscious awareness and perform that which is your purpose in the middle of stress.

I experienced this when I was engaged to a dear Soul who was diagnosed with a malignant brain tumor. Though the circumstances were grave, I was his caregiver to the end. I was able to draw upon the deep well of spiritual support from within me and from the many friends who hovered closely like angels.

Thriving is realized when you are open to every experience in life as a gift of awareness. Naturally, it can be felt when things are going well, when money is plentiful, when loved ones are kind, and when you feel "in the flow."

When I learned to thrive in uncertainty, life became a friend. Instead of feeling a victim of life's circumstances, I discovered that, if I choose to open to new learning and engage with the present moment as if it were a present wrapped and ready to be discovered, I really did prosper—even if I had not noticed it at the time. Prosperity has come to me in the form of friends, associates, and opportunities that I could never have dreamed of if I had not chosen to see uncertainty as the source of unlimited possibilities.

Like a balloon flying ever higher as we let go of the string, we can discover higher possibilities. Do we ever really have a firm hold of the string? I believe that a greater plan or synchronicity exists. If we get out of our own way, the outcomes are better than we could ever have planned for ourselves.

This has been proven to me over and over, but never more clearly than when my beloved husband showed up in my life. Just eleven months after burying my fiancé, along came the partner of my dreams. Not a perfect man, but a man who is perfect for me.

May you thrive as you let go of the string and discover possibilities greater than your dreams.

Wisdom from a Highway Sign

In all experience there is the consciousness of something which lies deeper than experience.

~ John Lancaster Spalding

ᜀᜆ᜔

While traveling along the freeway in rural south Jersey, I passed a sign that triggered a deep pondering and produced new awareness. It is funny how even the simplest everyday experience can bring out our inner wisdom.

The sign read: "If money is burning a hole in your pocket, it's not new pants that you need."

It flew past me too fast to read the small print below, which might have revealed the sponsor of the message. However, it was my perception of the message and not the intention of the sponsor that really mattered.

First, I thought, "Does money 'burn a hole' in my pocket?" Sometimes, yes. Have you ever felt the need to spend? In other words, have you ever been compelled to go shopping as a diversion or as an activity to take away boredom or unhappiness? I have.

One of my friend's self-worth is linked to the clothes she wears. Her time is spent on eBay, seeking out bargains, more and more bargains, buying more clothes than can be worn in a month. When we spend time and money soothing our ailing self-worth and unhappiness, we will never find real satisfaction or preserve a "nest egg" that offers security and resources for the future. We will find ourselves busily looking for healing in the wrong places.

The phrase "it's not new pants that you need" begs this question: "What is the deeper need when it seems that money burns a hole in your pocket?"

After reading my list, you could make a list of your own suggestions:

+ I need to count my blessings and value my relationships, recognizing that I have everything I really need in this moment.
+ I need to act to create healing for myself—like take a walk in the woods, soak in a bubble bath, fix a scrumptious meal, give a neck

massage to my beloved, or read an inspiring book—rather than try to spend my way to happiness.

+ I need to write down my personal goals and what resources I need to achieve them. Then I can prepare a budget to make it happen. Writing a plan brings a sense of empowerment.

+ I need to stop getting caught up in the never-ending search for happiness in things outside myself and find my own inner place of peace through meditation or contemplation.

All these thoughts came from a highway sign, which proves that whenever you are ready to learn, life will be your teacher, guiding you in the simplest ways. However, you first need to be open to viewing the experiences of your life as messages from your Divine Source, showing you the way to be happy.

Reflections of a Wandering Soul

We should give as we should receive, cheerfully, quickly and without hesitation; for there is no grace in a benefit that sticks to the fingers.

~ Seneca

❧ ❦

In 2006, my husband and I had the rare opportunity to take what we called our Alaskan Odyssey, a magnificent three-month driving and camping adventure. As our trip of a lifetime was nearing completion, I began to reflect on what had been gained from wandering about in the U.S. and Canada for three months.

I had been itching for a change. We were delighted that all our routines would be shattered. Yet, in truth, I found it difficult at first to manage the ever-changing locations and circumstances in which we found ourselves. The first thing I realized is that *change may not necessarily be easy even when you desire it!*

As days became weeks, I discovered particular enjoyment in traveling through the countryside near only small towns, if at all. There was an energetic difference between the sweet hum of nature and the buzz of the city.

Have you noticed how our large cities, with people living on top of each other, seem to produce frenetic lives? On the other hand, living within the wonders of nature and its processes encourages greater inner harmony and peace. *A spacious outer world seems to increase the chance of discovering our inner spaciousness.*

After two months on the road, being the "Great Observer" and enjoying sights and experiences that others only dream of, I felt uncomfortable. I was receiving so much from our experiences, but how much was I giving back? I was out of balance. It had been a long stretch without having given to others. My client schedule had been drastically reduced and I felt purposeless.

> *Giving and receiving are different sides of the same coin.*
> *When you do mostly giving or when you do mostly receiving,*
> *your life is not balanced.*

All things considered, the strongest feeling was gratitude for our three-month journey—the sights, the sounds, and the insights—and the opportunity to return home to be of service to my clients and a guide for charting their Soul's journeys.

Interrogating the Future

Let us be of good cheer, however, remembering that the misfortunes hardest to bear are those which never come.

~ James Russell Lowell

࿊

It is curious that we humans spend so much time pondering the future that we can miss the happiness and clues for fulfillment in the present moment. Recently, I caught myself feeling anxiety about what might happen in the next couple of days.

It was not that anything planned was unpleasant; quite the contrary. Why then did I feel anxious? When I dug deeper, I realized that I wanted to be sure everything happened just as I had planned. My worry was about the unknown. What if "that" happened? What if "that" *didn't* happen? Oh, my!

I started thinking about how often I "interrogate the future." That is, I question what *might* happen, fearful that what *will* happen might derail my well-dreamed-of expectations of the way it ought to be.

However, what happens or doesn't happen in the future isn't always something to fear.

How many times has life transformed mysteriously and wonderfully without the aid of any preconceived notions? Surprise events—like gifts from the Good Fairy, finding my comfortable home, encountering a fascinating new friend, and receiving invitations to speak—have appeared to enrich my life. I did not need to know about them ahead of time to benefit from and enjoy them. Even when the unexpected appeared at first to be dreadful, in time I usually grew to realize the underlying gift of evolutionary growth that came from it.

Noticing my anxiety brings the awareness that I want to control my life or believe I know what is best for me. However, I don't always consciously know what is best. My role is to imagine or intend what I would like, but then let it go and gratefully receive whatever enters my life as a gift of what is best for the next step in my life's journey.

This topic is quite appropriate right now because, in the next few years, the rate of breakdown of old ways brought about by innovations and change is likely to accelerate. We all will need to beware of "interrogating the future" when feeling fear and trepidation about the unknown.

Rather than worry about the future, it is best to put your focus on being mindful of all that you have in this present moment. Are you healthy? Are you fed? Are you clothed and warm? Do you give and receive love? If the answers are yes, then you are better off than many others.

I know of no better way to prime the pump of abundance and happiness than to appreciate what you already have in this moment. Open up to the mystery and miracle that is present in your life right here and now.

The Price of Freedom Includes Letting Go

Give to every other human being every right that you claim for yourself.

~ Robert Ingersoll

ॐॐ

In the U.S., we talk a lot about freedom. We pride ourselves on being the "land of the free and the home of the brave." Our freedoms are protected by the Constitution, yet our freedom has not been free. Many lives have been lost defending our freedom.

Freedom has another cost rarely talked about and yet worthy of consideration: *the need to let go*. What do I mean by that?

In a free society, you have to *let go* of the illusion that you can control others' opinions and values. As a result of our revolution against English rule, we chose to leave behind monarchs who would control us.

In a free society, we have to *let go* of assuming our answer is the right answer. Everyone's opinion is right for them—and they are entitled to express it. You may have to give up having your way. When the majority rules, you may not always be in the majority.

How does this work in everyday life? If you want freedom of expression in your home, you need to *let go* of being the only one to have a say and listen to what others think. If you wish to be free to do whatever you want, you'll have to give up control of other people's time.

If you want more free time, you will surely need to *let go* of some commitments to make time. If you would like to be free to travel the world, you will need to *let go* of some of your material possessions.

On a deeper level, a free-spirited person will *let go* of worries, judgments, and attachments. Freedom comes when we *let go* into a place of trust in the goodness that is God.

Trusting the wisdom of the whole populace is also needed to maintain the freedom found in democracy, for wisdom lies in everyone and in no one person alone. It definitely takes all voices for wisdom to be found.

Chapter 2
Expanding Self-awareness

Go on a journey from self to Self, my friend...
Such a journey transforms the earth into a mine of gold.

~ Julaluddin Rumi

The Benefits of Being Yourself

People travel to wonder at the height of the mountains, at the huge waves of the seas, at the long course of the rivers, at the vast compass of the ocean, at the circular motion of the stars, and yet they pass by themselves without wondering.

~ St. Augustine

❧❧

You might find this a strange title since, conceivably, we really have no choice. Like me, many people have spent years trying to be someone else who is better looking, smarter, more accomplished, or more likeable. Being your own self may not always have been acceptable to others as you grew up. Sadly, the self-criticism that comes from idealizing other people erodes your confidence and comfort with who you really are.

When you finally realize that being yourself is the only thing you can do, relief and deep joy follow!

I am not suggesting that we can't set self-improvement goals and achieve them. In truth, however, our essential being is so incredibly unique and special that looking at others and trying to become like someone else you admire is a project doomed to failure.

When you compare yourself to external criteria, you negate the joy of being fully and completely yourself!

What are the benefits of being your authentic self?

First, you are free from unnatural self-improvement efforts. When you look at someone you admire, you can send them a "thank-you" thought. Since they are who they are, you don't have to be them. You can simply be free to be yourself!

Second, by being yourself, you are likely to discover that the people attracted to you are the people you really like. Your essential self, no longer blocked by self-criticism, draws kindred Souls to you—people who have similar likes and dislikes and, most of all, people who appreciate you just as you are.

Third, when you are comfortable with being who you are, you may discover that others—even those who are very different than you—are more acceptable to you. There is less of an urge to criticize or find fault with those who are different. When we are most critical of ourselves, we are also most critical of others.

Surely there are other benefits. May you discover them by being just who you are!

The Importance of Self-care

Self-love, my liege, is not so vile a sin as self-neglecting.

~ Shakespeare in *Henry V*

ॐ✍

In the world in which I was raised, emphasis was given to caring for others. I was the oldest of six children with a mother who was often overwhelmed. Service to the needs of others became as natural as breathing. It still is. Does this sound familiar?

Through the years, however, I have come to realize the importance and absolute necessity of self-care if you intend to provide good service in the world.

In truth, unless you are feeling empowered and energized in your own life, you won't have the inner resources to give to others; worse, resentment will underlie whatever you do give.

Self-care can mean different things to different people. Everyone will take a unique approach to personal satisfaction. You may find enjoyment by a walk in the woods; another may feel soothed by a visit to a day spa; I find being by a body of water very healing.

Doing whatever replenishes and rejuvenates you *is not selfish*. It is self-loving and part of the self-care we each need to maintain our contentment with ourselves and our lives.

Self-care activities may be physical (jogging), emotional (a day at the art museum), or spiritual (a long meditation by the water). It doesn't matter. This will be unique to you and come from where you personally draw your inspiration and energy for living.

How well have you been maintaining your needed self-care lately? Particularly if you have a focus of service to others, you must not disregard your own needs.

Self-care is actually a means for giving clear and useful service in the world. It helps keep our lives in balance—something we all need to do.

Self-criticism: Who's Voice Is It?

Criticism is prejudice made plausible.

~ H. L. Mencken

❧❦

Many of us are haunted by persistent, self-critical thoughts like, "What makes you think you can do that? You'll never do it right? What if you fail?"

It doesn't matter whether you have already proved yourself as capable in a particular arena. The inertia generated by self-critical thoughts can leave you paralyzed and unwilling to step forward to act, when you might just as easily be successful and disprove those thoughts.

Self-criticism is often the cause of depression, apathy, immobilization, and a general lack of direction. Have you stopped to think who is doing the criticizing? Who determined that you are not good enough? Who said you never do it right? Who said you are sure to fail?

As children, we are influenced by a variety of caregivers who probably had a sincere desire to nurture and guide us toward adulthood (as they perceived it, of course). They left us with subtle (or not so subtle) messages about our abilities that stuck with us, buried securely in our subconscious. We internalized them as "truths" and our actions have been controlled by them ever since. However, they were merely personal opinions and biases that our caregivers passed on to us.

For example, I remember being told, "You have no artistic talent." After that, whenever there was an opportunity to get involved in creative activities of any kind, I avoided it. My critical inner voice told me I could not be creative and so I was not.

This influence can also be positive. When I was told "You have a good head on your shoulders," I developed confidence in my mental abilities. Unfortunately, it has taken much of my life to awaken my creative expression so it could work in concert with my intellect.

One day, I heard a voice in my mind, running me down and saying that I wasn't worthy or capable. Pondering the voice and what it said, I recognized that I was letting my father's voice from the past control me. All this time, under the spell of subconscious programming, I had been limited by a voice from the past—not the voice of my Inner Self. In a moment of grace, as I became aware of the voice, I shouted out, "No, no! That's not true and I won't believe it!"

That awareness produced a noticeable shift in my self-confidence around that particular issue. Now, when I feel uncertain due to self-critical thoughts, I listen and discern whose voice is speaking and quiz myself as to whether I really believe the criticism I am hearing.

There may be times when your own conscience has valid points to make, but that doesn't usually appear as destructive self-criticism. It is more likely heard, for example, as suggestions for doing better the next time or ideas to improve your performance, like good advice.

Try it! Next time you become aware of an inner self-critical voice, consider who is speaking and decide if you agree that it is really true.

Self-doubt: a Form of Abuse

The only limit to our realization of tomorrow will be our doubts of today.

~ Franklin Delano Roosevelt

➳∾⬅

On the road to a happier, more fulfilling life, you will have to slay the demon of self-doubt. Why? It is clearly a form of self-abuse.

We have all suffered under self-doubt at some time in our lives. Those nagging thoughts—"You are not good enough," "You can't do that," "You are not smart enough, wise enough, or attractive enough"—abuse your sense of self-worth and well-being.

The origin of this abuse, as I have already stated, lies within the voices we heard in our early years. Often due to *their* insecurities, the words of our parents and early authority figures caused us to question our own instincts and made us believe that what we desired was not possible.

It could have been as simple as someone making an idle comment. Unfortunately, that comment stuck with us and colored our view of ourselves from then on. In my case, I had a teacher who said I had "no artistic ability." For more than 20 years, I doubted my creative ability until I woke up to the reality that it was not true.

What example can you find in your own life? Perhaps an overcautious mother convinced you that you were not physically capable of competing athletically. The possible false beliefs established in that way are limitless.

Of course, those authority figures from the past probably did not mean to abuse you. They were merely operating out of their own fears and limitations.

However, the self-doubt that you continue to hold inside is now a form of ongoing self-abuse. It prevents you from trying to reach your goals, and stops you from believing that you deserve to be happy and fulfilled.

Ironically, some of the most compassionate and caring people can be the harshest self-critics.

If you are the kind of person who is willing to encourage and support others, what is stopping you from supporting yourself? Become your own cheerleader! Erase those nagging doubts by replacing them with positive affirmations.

While you are at it, you can also do yourself a favor by surrounding yourself with supportive friends and colleagues who believe in you and offer generous encouragement. Anyone you associate with who doesn't see the best in you is only adding to your self-abuse. Change your friends if necessary.

Make it a high priority to be an encouraging friend to yourself by putting an end to abusing, self-doubting thoughts.

How Would My Life Be Different If …

Tension is who you think you should be. Relaxation is who you are.

~ Japanese proverb

❧ ❦

Do you have a longstanding issue in your life that drains your energy, like a hole in a tire, or covers your joy, like a wet blanket? Unbelievably, I have spent 90 percent of the last 50 years disgusted with my body and worried about my weight.

Being familiar with body self-hate, you can imagine how shocked I was when, while showering, I heard an inner voice ask, "How would your life be different if you no longer had to worry about your body?"

That was a shocking question! Have you been burdened by self-criticism of some aspect of yourself? Mine is my weight. Yours could be anything.

What if we just gave up the story, the struggle, and the complaint?

That is what I pondered. I had lost 30 pounds over a six-month period and was as close to normal weight as I had been in many years. I felt good, people (and my hubby) said I looked good, and I had returned to yoga.

Yet, even at a comfortable weight—or perhaps because of it—I noticed how much of my day was spent thinking about what I ate, how I looked, whether my clothes fit right, *blah, blah, blah* …

What a waste of energy! At my age, it is just not important anymore. I have a partner who loves me and my body (even when I weighed more). So why do I torture myself?

It is the "monkey mind". The "monkey mind" is like a machine that, once programmed, perpetuates the same function until something comes along to reprogram it. Fortunately, the voice of my Inner Self had interrupted the programming by asking a question that opened up new awareness.

I began to consider how my life would be different if I didn't obsess about my body all day. What came to mind was that I would be free to create, imagine, and explore new ideas, possibilities, and actions.

From that realization, I decided that I would stop every time I become aware of another "body thought" and replace it with a positive thought about myself (e.g., something I had done that benefited another). I refused to waste any more energy on the state of my weight.

Got something you'd like to reprogram? Replace a negative thought with a positive one and love yourself.

Imperfections as Part of Life's Plan

It is only imperfection that complains of what is imperfect. The more perfect we are the more gentle and quiet we become towards the defects of others.

~ Joseph Addison

❧ ❧

How might you live differently if you realized that what you have perceived as imperfections were actually part of your Soul's plan for your life? I am aware, as I ponder this for my own life, that this is no simple question.

Born with a deep inner desire for perfection, when I feel I don't measure up to my own standards, I can drown myself in criticism—a criticism much harsher that anyone else would ever express.

Am I alone in this self-criticism? I don't think so.

Could it be, however, that our inner desire for perfection is better understood as a compass pointing in the direction of our greatest good and towards an opportunity for personal growth?

What if we were never meant to be stymied by self-criticism or deterred by self-doubt?

Here's something you could try: When you feel a sudden disappointment in yourself—perhaps you've fallen short of your goal in some way or there was an unintended outcome from something you did or said—stop *before* you fall into despair.

Think to yourself, "What a gift this is! I am now aware of what doesn't work. I have more information with which to redirect my behavior and choose to act differently next time around."

The blessing of awareness that comes from discovering my imperfections gives me the opportunity to make a course correction as a result.

Romans chapter 8 in the Bible says, "All things work together for good." Our imperfections are benevolent gifts that show us the way to self-improvement. Bless them as you bless yourself for seeking to improve and perfect yourself!

Befriending Our Problems

Crisis is the dangerous breaking of glass that opens locked windows of opportunity that require perceptiveness and courage to move through, with care.

~ Tom Atlee, Co-Intelligence Institute

❧

For many of us, worries about the economic and political scene (e.g., the stock market, healthcare and the federal deficit) and fear of an unknown future have our blood pressure rising along with our credit card debt. Fear has become a powerful tool for all sides to wield in the public debate, while entrenched polarization ensures that nothing moves forward.

At the same time, more and more people are seeking to use pharmaceuticals to treat their depression, thinking that drugs are the answer to maintaining functionality, while avoiding the cause and ignoring the signal that something is wrong.

Clearly, when we look out at the world, *what appears to be broken and needs to be fixed is everywhere.* There is an intersection between our own psychological and spiritual health and the actual landscape of our lives.

Tom Atlee of the Co-Intelligence Institute has observed that "... evolution, like water behind a dam, knows where all the cracks are, and is working on them right now with increasing intensity."

Could it be that something new is trying to happen, seeking the transformation of the Whole? Might our out-of-balance world be due to increased spiritual energy seeking to awaken the values of the heart—compassion, generosity, forgiveness, and a desire to live in harmony with others?

I propose that the only way forward through this minefield is to *befriend our problems as the messengers that they are,* highlighting the empty, loveless, or meaningless places in our lives that thirst for something meaningful and real.

When we anxiously hold onto the way things were—and want no disruptions in our lives—we avoid finding answers since the current status quo is closely tied to the malaise on the planet.

I remember being surprised years ago when I read *Care of the Soul* by Thomas Moore. He titled one of the chapters "The Gift of Depression." I had to think about that.

What if we learned to suffer more effectively? Rather than failing to notice the opportunities and lessons our challenges offer, we could see the problem and the solution as two sides of the same coin.

In fact, today's suffering could become tomorrow's happiness. Who would you be today if it weren't for your suffering? Think back. Wasn't there a jewel of awareness and growth offered in almost every tribulation?

Regardless of whether society is ready to transform, individuals who bring their lives into balance and harmony—restoring the love, hope, and unity that is their birthright—actually aid the possibilities for change in the wider world.

We could, as Tom Atlee suggests, "use our differences and our challenges creatively, not simply as problems to avoid or solve, but as signs of new life pushing to emerge—and as invitations into a new, more whole tomorrow."

In the next few years, remember that these invitations will be of the utmost importance. Profound changes are ahead; whether we move forward gracefully, or kick and scream, depends on our ability to see problems as friends. Let go of the past.

Accept the opportunity offered by crisis rather than fear the unknown.

Step Up to the Mirror and Own the Love

Happiness is looking at a mirror and liking what you see.

~ Anonymous

৵◌৶

Clients and friends who know about my relationship with my husband, Chuck, often ask me how I got so lucky. It is true that I am blessed with a partner who is affectionate, generous, and deeply spiritual, but I always tell them, "Relationships are not so much about the other person as they are about you."

How can that be? Aren't you looking for the "right mate"? Isn't it important to find the "right one"? In my experience, the issue is not *finding* the right mate; that will happen naturally. It is more important to *be* the right mate.

All relationships begin and end with you. If you are not open to sharing yourself honestly and openly, and if you question whether you are worthy of love, there is no one who will ever be able to storm the walls or convince you to receive the love they offer. Begin the deep work of erasing all the critical voices from past relationships (e.g., parents, teachers, or intimates). Love and accept yourself just as you are—imperfect, but still growing.

After all, how can you expect someone else to love you if you can't love yourself? When your relationship with yourself is healthy, you are able to look upon another person with acceptance for their human frailties and discover the unique qualities that make them attractive—or at least interesting—rather than troubling.

When you struggle with unloved parts of yourself, it is easy to project them onto others. Our relationships can be thought of as mirrors on which we project our unhealed wounds. We may not be aware we are doing it, so we blame the other person for what we see in them while they are simply reflecting the unhealed part of ourselves.

When challenges arise due to differing points of view, rather than blaming the other person, I suggest you "step up to the mirror" presented by the person with whom you disagree.

Discuss the situation with the other person as if you were talking to a different part of yourself, and use the same love and acceptance you would give to yourself. Open to discovering what the other person is feeling; you may be surprised how quickly tension is defused and solutions appear. In this way, you will "own the love."

"Step up to the mirror" in your past and present, whether that is easy or challenging. "Own the love" by honor yourself and accepting the differences.

Comparing Yourself to Others

Love is the total absence of fear. Love asks no questions. Its natural state is one of extension and expansion, not comparison and measurement.

~ Gerald Jampolsky

☙ ❧

The greatest barrier to our personal joy and peace is comparing who we are to others. Our rational mind is always sorting sensory input and categorizing it by comparison and contrast (e.g., "That person is skinnier than I," "That person is smarter than I," or "That person is _____ than I"—you fill in the blank).

The trouble lies not in the comparison but in the beliefs and values we hold about needing to measure up to or "win" in that comparison. Who says we need to be thinner or smarter than anyone else? If we were living in Renaissance Europe in the days of the artist Rubens, being thinner would be shameful and an indication of poverty.

The trouble with comparing your mental capability with others is that there will always be someone smarter. No matter what topic you choose, there is an expert with greater knowledge.

Different cultures have a different value for achievement. Some cultures place a strong emphasis on educational achievement; other cultures may prize woodworking skills or creative talents.

The wondrous range of topics for which there are experts—from astrophysics to zoology—excites me. However, if everyone excelled at medicine, who would repair my car?

No matter what level of school you have achieved, it is only when you apply what you have learned in real-life situations that it has any value. Knowledge is what we learn from books or others, but wisdom comes from personal application of that "book learning."

Therefore, if you find your inner critic has in any way compared you negatively to another, *don't listen*. Remember to honor your own wisdom gained from putting what you've learned into practical application.

Clearly, the measures we use to compare ourselves to others are culturally biased and subject to change, and are meaningless to the Truth of who we really are. Our intrinsic worth or value simply cannot be measured against anyone else and doesn't change through eternity.

Each of us is as unique as a snowflake, as rare as a diamond, and one of a kind!

As an astrologer, I have discovered this truth again and again. When my clients describe their life experiences and choices, I am filled with awe at the wondrous variety. The ways each individual contributes to and lives life are magnificently unique!

Put Your Own Mask on First

You must love yourself before you love another. By accepting yourself and joyfully being what you are, you fulfill your own abilities, and your simple presence makes others happy.

~ Jane Roberts

❧

The complexities and demands of living often lead to stress. The responsibilities of maintaining a job and caring for a family can be a challenge to balance. Mothers with small children are particularly vulnerable to spending their energy for the benefit of everyone but themselves. However, being overcommitted with no time for personal interests is by no means a gender-defined issue. Stress can visit everyone.

Have you ever found yourself saying "yes" to a request from someone and later find you resent that you were even asked?

If you have a compassionate, cooperative, and caring nature, you may be particularly vulnerable to this malady. It feels good when you help out, but the reality of "just so much time available" limits what is possible.

My youngest daughter was struggling with this issue and shared her new awareness with me. (Have you ever noticed how wise your children are when you take the time to listen?)

Aboard a plane bound for home, feeling very drained and pondering the weight of all her responsibilities, the flight attendant gave the safety instructions. At the part when the safety message refers to a possible loss of cabin pressure, she heard the flight attendant say, as if for the first time, "Mothers with children: put your mask on first and then assist your children."

In a flash, she realized that mothers need to put their mask on first so they are capable of assisting their children. She decided that, when she finds herself overloaded with responsibilities, it is time to "put her mask on first." That realization has given her permission to take care of herself so she will have more of herself to give to others.

Remember: Your own well-being is important if you want to have the energy and enthusiasm to be of service to others.

Put your mask on first!

Are You Living Authentically?

If you call forth what is in you, it will save you. If you do not call forth what is in you, it will destroy you.

~ Gospel of St. Thomas

☙❧

Do you consider yourself the "author" of your life? If not, then you may not be living authentically. That is, you may be living the life your family, your spouse, or your boss thinks you should, but you are not living true to your own inner prompting.

There are several ways this could show up. Have you ever said "yes" when you really didn't want to, for fear that the other person would think badly about you? When you shop for clothes, are you worried about whether it is a style that is acceptable to your friends? Do you avoid starting a conversation with a stranger because you are unsure if what you say would be welcome? Worrying about what others think prevents us from living authentically (i.e., from being our true selves).

You are a unique individual. Since no one has ever had the same life experiences you have had, or expressed all the talents you do, or looked out of your eyes with your point of view, there is no one who has any right to judge you.

No one has the ability to really know you completely, thus they don't have any basis to judge you (nor do you have any basis to judge them).

Sadly, when we are vigilantly paying attention to what others think and deny our authentic Self, we are being dishonest. That's when I think we have it all wrong.

Instead of wondering what others think, we ought to turn our focus around. Being caring and responsive to the needs of others, or simply showing interest in their lives rather than being anxious that we are not measuring up, is the way to live authentically—as the "author" of our lives.

Since there is no one else like you in the whole universe, if you are not playing your unique role, the universe is incomplete and out of sync. The world, to be complete, needs you to be authentically behaving, contributing, and expressing just who you are.

If you feel that you are not always behaving authentically, change direction. In other words, don't let someone else hold the key to whether you are right or wrong, good or bad. Choose to operate from you own inner heart's authentic expression. Choose to give yourself praise when due and encouragement for improving yourself when that is necessary.

To maintain your authentic Self, it comes easier if you spend time listening to your inner feelings—what I call your heart's voice. It can be done by taking a walk in the woods or sitting quietly in meditation. I find that spending enough time alone is absolutely essential to being authentic in my daily life.

Remembering Why

Growth of the soul is our goal, and there are many ways to encourage that growth, such as through love, nature, healing our wounds, forgiveness, and service. The soul grows well when giving and receiving love. I nourish my soul daily by loving others and being vulnerable to their love. Love is, after all, a verb, an action word, not a noun.

~ Joan Borysenko, Ph.D.

❧ ❧

The winter holiday season is notoriously filled with hustle and bustle. There are gifts to buy, decorations to make or purchase, parties to attend or give, groceries to buy, and special recipes to prepare. Without a doubt, our "to-do" lists are longer at this time of the year than any other.

Stress and frustration may accompany tasks such as balancing your checkbook or struggling with wrapping paper. At these times, all the joy seems to fade, and you may end up wanting to avoid the whole thing completely.

When you feel stressed, stop for a moment *to consider... Why* am I doing what I am doing?"

Are you feverishly buying gifts, selecting just the right color or size to please a loved one? Recognize that, underneath the tension, you feel there is a reason you are doing it. Enjoy what you are doing. Enjoy the task of shopping and revel in the possibility of pleasing Aunt Susie with your choice. Imagine her face as she opens your package.

Are you anxious about what to buy? Are you worried about your purchase? Have you allowed yourself to feel obligated? Are you caught up in the "tit for tat" measuring of whether you spent as much on someone as they spent on you? What is your motivation for buying?

When you find yourself harried and hassled with too much to do and too little time to do it (this could be at any time of the year), stop and remember why you are doing what you are doing. If love is the reason—and it is theoretically the center focus of the season—why aren't you feeling loving and joyful? What can you do to change your experience?

At a stressful moment, stop and ponder. Remembering "why" may inspire you with new energy.

If you don't like the reason you come up with, then don't do it! You may be following a tradition that no longer has meaning. The stress may come from performing old, meaningless, and empty rituals. If that is true, then by all means let go and do something new that does have meaning.

Remembering "why" can revitalize the significance of your actions and refocus you toward love and joy. Let love be your guide and the season will flourish with the energies of peace and joy.

Choosing Between Love and Fear

The only thing we have to fear is fear itself.

~ Franklin D. Roosevelt

❧❦

Ever since the events of September 11, 2001, it seems that fear is pervasive. It is true the actions of that day were never anticipated. Americans lived for decades without fear of foreign attack.

Since then, the possibility of attack—any time, any place—has become a constant reality, fed by the news and Homeland Security's persistent color-coded alarms. In short, we are constantly reminded that we should be fearful, to the detriment of the health of our body, mind, and Soul.

In his book, *Love is Letting Go of Fear*, Gerald Jampolsky explains that when we are in a fearful state, love is blocked from our awareness. Yet, love is our true nature, the very thing we yearn to experience. What is all this paranoia doing to our collective well-being?

Our individual psyches do not thrive in an environment of fear, anger, and revenge. When these emotions are acted out on the world stage, it is more difficult for us to remember that love is our true nature.

If what is happening in the world is a reflection of our collective consciousness—and I believe that is true—then it is also a message for humanity's collective growth and evolution. All this fear in the atmosphere tells me that, underneath the paranoia, love is crying out to be realized and expressed. We are being called to a deeper understanding and expression of our loving nature.

To more fully express our loving nature, however, we need to consciously recognize when we are being fear-driven, when we have blocked our loving nature by falling prey to external fears. Fear's influence can manifest in subtle, very personal ways.

When I feel reluctant to go forward, based on past assumptions about whether something will work successfully, am I being controlled by fear? When I doubt my abilities or worry whether others are talking behind my back, I am likely to be under the spell of fear. The clue is that, whenever I feel contracted rather than open, I am likely to be bound up by fear.

Love, on the other hand, wants to fully engage in life, looking toward possibilities and knowing that every moment is new. *The past never writes the future.* Love opens up to everyone, embracing differences and seeking understanding of the other's perspective. Love creatively seeks to find points of agreement and knows that the world can work for everyone.

If that is true, what are some ways we could increase the expression of love in our relationships? Be alert to when you feel shut down and negative. Recognize when fear arises, and find ways to open to your own inner loving nature.

Remember: Fear constricts and love expands!

"Yes" Has No Meaning Without "No"

To know what you prefer, instead of humbly saying "Amen" to what the world says you ought to prefer, is to have kept your soul alive.

~ Robert Louis Stevenson

෨•෬

Ever since I stopped working in the "nine-to-five world," I have found no end to the good causes and helpful activities with which I could occupy my time. There are many worthy causes in the world as well as friends and neighbors I could help. Like me, you may have felt the stress that comes from wanting to help and yet not having enough hours in your day.

Whether it's a product of your upbringing—placing others' needs before your own—or just your natural giving nature, sooner or later you will end up needing to face the limits of time.

Whether we like it or not, all who dwell on Earth are subject to the limitation of time. Time is a boundary we must learn to respect, which is a good thing. Otherwise, we might not be discriminating about where we spend our precious time and energy. In order to prioritize and focus our efforts, it is necessary to realize when to say the "N" word: *no!*

"No, I can't. I have too much on my plate."

"No, my time is focused on ..."

Even when you have a naturally cheerful, can-do attitude, occasionally saying the opposite of "yes" is necessary to make progress on self-defined priorities. In fact, if you don't say "no" to something, your "yes" has no meaning—another of life's paradoxes.

If you were raised to be giving and caring toward others, like I was, the importance of saying "no" might come as a shock. However, until you become comfortable with setting a boundary around what you will do, you may be kind to others but feel resentful and used when you do. What about your own self-defined priorities?

Expanding your self-awareness is aided by discover the power of *no!*

Chapter 3
Embracing Relationships

*Security in a relationship lies neither in looking back
to what was in nostalgia,
nor forward to what it might be in dread or anticipation,
but living in the present relationship and accepting it as it is now.*

~ Anne Morrow Lindbergh

The Essence of Family

Call it a clan, call it a network, call it a tribe, call it a family. Whatever you call it, whoever you are, you need one.

~ Jane Howard

෨෪෫

While sitting in a rain-soaked campsite, enjoying the annual family campout with my two daughters, their families, and several others, I ponder the meaning of family. At that moment, my thoughts of family produced warm, nurturing feelings of belonging. However, I am no stranger to family-engendered feelings of anger, disappointment, and loneliness, such as I felt in my youth.

At some point, we must make sense of our relationships with family members. Were your family members supportive and encouraging or controlling and critical? Did you enjoy being with your family or did you want to get away? How are your relationships now?

There's no doubt that *family is important*. Within it lie the roots of who we are. Each of us has been molded by the environment in which we were born and has formed opinions and beliefs about life from our early experiences.

As we get older, we get the chance to rethink our childhood and perhaps see our parental figures in a new way. Their level of emotional maturity becomes easier to assess when we have attained an adult level of conscious awareness. Hopefully, by adulthood, we have had the chance to recognize that they did the best they could at the time, given who they were and the wounds of their own childhoods.

In her book, *Sacred Contracts*, Carolyn Myss introduces the idea that we may have chosen our parents. In fact, we may have "Soul contracts" with them (i.e., contracts to support each other's Soul journey) though not necessarily always in a harmonious way.

Perhaps the Creator designed the family experience for our evolutionary growth. Not only are we born into a family, most of us have created our own family, and everyone can be said to be part of the human family—the family of nations and of all beings. We are certainly designed to feel related to various groups as if they were family.

Family facilitates our self-discovery through the quality of our relationships with family members. Just as "no man is an island," it is also true that no man (or woman) can function well without a family.

Where do you find your most beneficial experience of family? If you come from a loving, supportive family, you most likely see them as the source of your love and belonging.

However, you may have unresolved issues and blocks from your family of origin. You may have found a sense of family within your friendships. Forming family-like ties with friends permits you to choose only those who offer support and understanding to belong to your clan. With friends, you may receive the same love and sense of belonging that others find within their blood ties.

Whether you find belonging among your blood family or among your friends, I believe it is still a precious and important experience that mirrors who we are and how we relate to others.

Either way, family is a gift that helps us grow and evolve, even through negative experiences. For example, the simple act of pushing back from parental judgments has strengthened my sense of uniqueness and my worth, which in turn has allowed me to follow my Soul's calling.

Consider the value of your family and the gifts they have given you. Tell them you appreciate the important role they have played in your life. Celebrate the contribution of family in your life.

Shattering Childhood Views of Powerlessness

Becoming a leader is synonymous with becoming yourself. It is precisely that simple, and it's also that difficult… First and foremost, find out what you're about and be that.

~ Warren Bennis, organizational development author

❧ ❧

As a child, my dad was the most powerful person in the world—my world. In any circumstance (e.g., what I ate, when I went to bed, with whom I could play), he had the final say. I learned early that power was a force outside of me that I would do best to respect and obey.

As I became more self-aware and self-directed, I learned that power comes in many forms, all of which have only the influence over me that I allow. People and circumstances have power over me only to the extent that I let them; if I do let them, it is because of my fear.

Without fear, nothing has power over me. It follows then that I am the source of any power—even external power—since I decide whether to fear it or not. Even laws have no power beyond the consent of the governed.

When my father (now getting up in age) recently shared some fears of his own, I was astounded. This new information was totally inconsistent with my childhood view of my father's power. From my perspective, he was always bold and fearless.

Although I long ago stopped fearing him and seeking his approval, this revelation was like discovering that the Wizard of Oz had no power. Instead of being a wizard, as I had believed, he was really only a human being. However, rather than feeling disappointed, it only deepened my love for him.

How many other places in my life have I given away my power to those who appeared more powerful, when in reality their power was a result of my own immature perception?

Where have you given away your power due to fear? Is it time to acknowledge the powerful person you are? Do you understand that all power actually originates from *within* you?

Victimhood

Self-pity is easily the most destructive of the non-pharmaceutical narcotics; it is addictive, gives momentary pleasure and separates the victim from reality.

~ John W. Gardner

❦

There is a strange phenomenon that occurs when something we are not expecting or do not like happens. I have watched myself react as if I had been attacked, betrayed, or singled out for punishment. I adopt the role of victim.

Naturally, every victim has to have a perpetrator: "I am a victim of _____" (fill in your favorite perpetrator). My favorites are life, the universe, or even God, but my closest loved ones are the easiest to blame.

The bottom line is that when we allow ourselves to feel like a victim, we have disempowered ourselves. No longer are we in charge of our lives, but are instead subject to the actions of another. Feeling like a victim is the ultimate self-inflicted put-down.

What is the source of those happenings that we think came from somewhere else and not from ourselves? Is the cause a friend or foe? Could it be possible that our conscious mind is unable to understand the benevolence underlying the happening? Why then do we so readily explain it by imagining that we are a victim of some person or force? Could there be unconscious forces that our Soul set in motion?

Some would say that, through astrology, we become more susceptible to victimhood because cosmic forces could be said to cause the unasked-for event. However, as an astrologer who believes we co-create with the Divine, I suggest that we are not a "victim" of the stars. Astrology helps decipher the synchronicity of the moment, allowing us to exercise our free will through informed and intelligent choices.

We do not need to be victims (i.e., people who are unaware or unwilling to take responsibility for their life by using what happens as guidance for navigating their path ahead). We take responsibility for directing our lives's path by using our ability to choose.

When something unexpected or unpleasant happens, don't become a victim. Choose how you will respond and thus "make lemonade out of lemons."

Privacy is Impossible and Undesirable

Look outside of the narrow focus we all get caught up in and see that whether you live in Aspen or in Africa, underneath we are all the same.

~ John Denver

༁

Privacy issues are a hot topic these days. Everywhere you turn, a new password is needed. Identity fraud, phishing, and spamming are now common threats. Even the government is rumored to have everyone's vital information in a database "to protect you."

From the point of view of a spiritual being living a human existence, is it really possible to maintain privacy? In the truest sense, privacy is not only impossible but it would be detrimental to your Soul's Journey if it were possible.

Now, don't freak out just yet! Stay with me a moment and let me share what I mean.

When we look out at the world of form, we see bodies that are different from each other; however, physicists tell us that, on a fundamental level, everything is basically energy vibrating at different rates. In a world that is pure energy, nothing is really solid. Living in this ever-changing energy that flows through our thoughts, emotions, and actions, we are constantly influencing and being influenced by others and our surroundings.

If that is true, then my thoughts about you radiate out and interact with you. On some level, whether consciously (telepathically) or unconsciously, your thoughts about me also influence me. Some people are more sensitive than others and are able to access subtle energies for information.

I believe that we are constantly sending out messages on energy wavelengths. It is an illusion to think that we can keep things inside ourselves. If that is true, what password could we possibly find that would be able to lock up the privacy of our thoughts?

From another perspective, if we seek to grow in our awareness of our connections with all of life—Oneness—why would we want to remain private? Wouldn't we want to be "known"?

Our fears and insecurities motivate our overwhelming need to maintain privacy. Our fears and insecurities also keep us separated from the awareness of our Oneness with all life.

It is my conscious desire to dissolve any feeling of separation and move toward the joy-filled awareness of connection with everything. I desire less privacy and more love.

Complete privacy is impossible—and undesirable—if you are seeking to dissolve fear-based separation and move into a deeper awareness of love in your life. There's nothing to lose and everything to gain as you open to connect rather than stay hidden.

Find the Confluence

The unlike is joined together, and from differences results the most beautiful harmony.

~ Heraclitus

☙❧

With all of the recent polarization (e.g., in the news, in the legislative process, and even interpersonally), how can we move forward or find harmony when we are locked in disagreements? When there is such great polarization, no progress and no harmony are possible.

How do we move forward, find solutions for our problems, and create new possibilities when those in government are acting like two prizefighters, bouncing around in opposite corners of the ring, waiting to come out and clobber each other?

In the personal realm, how does any relationship continue when, in an argument, each member digs in their heels and won't budge? Divorces are often made of such behavior. I have had one of those myself and, yes, it was because we both were in separate corners in our own minds.

I hold an image of two rivers, the headwaters of each originating in very different climes, which flow toward a place of meeting—a "confluence." From that point, they merge and become a single awesome, powerful river that enriches land for miles around.

How can we find that meeting place—the confluence of our separateness—where our differences bring blessings to the outcomes based on finding common ground?

To start, we will not find the confluence by holding to the idea of "right" versus "wrong." Life is too complex to be boiled down to just two truths. Right and wrong are completely situational. What is right in one situation is often wrong for another. In the end, we can't know what is right for another, but only what is right for ourselves.

Confluence can only be found by opening up to more than we already know. We might need to accept that all the wisdom in the world does not reside in our brains. If we accept this, we have the opportunity to discover new information that possibly reveals new common ground.

Common ground is what paves the way to agreements. Agreements move us toward progress and harmony. It is so simple to talk about, but not so simple to discover while we still think we are "right."

Is there someone in your life with whom you don't see eye to eye? What if you stopped defending your position and started asking questions about their position, why they feel that way, and how they got there? You'd be surprised how quickly the tension defuses. As a result, it becomes much easier to find the confluence. This is a process that my husband and I use whenever our inevitable differences in opinion appear.

Wistfully, I dream of convincing the rest of the world to work diligently toward common ground, but then I remember we can only fix ourselves by taking responsibility for how we behave in our own lives and seek the confluence of our lives's rivers with the rivers of others!

Who is There to Blame?

When nothing is judged, there is nothing to forgive.

~ Anonymous

જ્જ

We probably learned the meaning of "blame" from our families. If my brother got hurt while we were playing, he would run to my mother and I would be blamed (sometimes rightly and sometimes wrongly). From my family, I learned that, when something does not go the way you want it, you should complain about it and find someone to blame.

What do we really get out of blaming others? We might think that blame places the responsibility for whatever happened on someone else, so we end up being supposedly "blameless."

However, blaming someone else leaves us powerless. In the act of blaming, we fail to take responsibility for our own life and act like a victim of others. That may have been okay when we were children; as adults, we should have learned that we create our own reality based on behavior for which we agree to be responsible (e.g., work, home, and relationships).

What if someone really does hurt me? Are they not to blame? Of course, they may be seen as the cause of our hurt, but what good does assigning blame really do? Does it make the hurt go away? Not really. It only keeps you thinking that you are a victim without the power to direct your own life.

If someone physically hurts me, I learned early to head in the opposite direction. There is no need to continue being hurt. If someone emotionally hurts me, I now consider whether the hurt I feel is due to unhealed or oversensitive feelings.

When you gather with others, especially family, beware of falling into the "blame game." What is gained from assigning blame for everything that happens?

Above all, let go of the blame from the past. Whatever hurts or disappointments onto which you continue to hold, sweep them into the dust bin of the past. Is it possible that whoever harmed you was doing the best they could at the time, considering their level of awareness?

Avoid potential conflict with others by simply acknowledging and permitting differences of opinion. Let your loved ones be who they are *and* give yourself permission to hold a different point of view. Love them anyway. Enjoy family conversations without the need to agree or assign blame.

* * *

As 2004 ended, the whole planet was reeling from the massive loss of life and destruction caused by the tsunami, which was touched off by an earthquake off the coast of Indonesia and swept across the Indian Ocean, devastating parts of 11 countries.

When something of this magnitude happens, we are challenged to make sense of it all. There was no one at which we could point a finger and no ideology out to get us. There was simply no one to blame. What leaps of mind help us reconcile the horror?

Some said the cause was ecological; that Mother Nature has had enough of mankind's abuse and was talking back. Others saw proof of a beginning to the prophesied "end times." Since the region affected was largely Muslim, some righteous Christians went so far as to say that God was declaring what side He is on.

True, the tsunami caused great suffering, but the event brought more than that. After the initial shock, there were numerous stories of miraculous rescues and open-hearted kindness. The relief response was unprecedented as almost every nation came forward with material and financial support—governments as well as private citizens.

For a couple of weeks, the 20-year Sri Lankan civil war was set aside as people were rescued and treated, regardless of their religious or political persuasion. The tsunami did not attack one particular religion or political view. It was an "equal opportunity" crisis.

What if, just as a turtle outgrows his shell, the quake and tsunami are part of the natural process of growth on planet Earth?

It is quite significant that, although quakes and tsunamis are not new and have been creating devastation for eons, this was the first time the whole world saw the damage on television and, as a result, was able to respond with help.

Perhaps, as a result of this trauma, we have increased our awareness that we are all one. As we respond by helping others, we reinforce the Truth that we are all in this together ... because we are.

Picking at the Wounds of Another

Everything that irritates us about others can lead us to an understanding of ourselves.

~ Carl Jung

❧ ❧

Recently, a friend (let's call her Sue) called to vent about a mutual friend (let's call her Jane). After a several-minute tirade of complaints, I began to feel uncomfortable. Sue's description of Jane's behavior was probably accurate, but why was it such a big deal? Why was Sue picking at Jane's wounds?

Though I also had experienced the same behavior from Jane, I understood that it was simply evidence of Jane's wounded self-image: She desperately needed everyone's attention focused on her.

I accept that, while everyone (including me) has been harmed and carries a primal wound, some people's wounds are deeper than others. Those who are courageous and determined may heal their wounds or at least begin to use them in a positive way.

Our wounds or vulnerabilities also have the potential to become strengths or gifts that we offer others. The person who has felt a lack of belonging is more likely to be welcoming to others.

Sue's challenge was in maintaining her own self-confidence, which is why Jane's grandstanding behavior was such a source of irritation.

I have learned that, when I get a strong reaction to someone's behavior, it is almost always because of my own unhealed wounds. Once aware of it, I reflect the focus back to me and spend time processing what caused my reaction. What wound in me is being projected onto someone else?

You might ask, "Is it really always about me?" I say yes! Your mind is always making interpretations—not based on the abstract reality of what you see but on the supposed meaning you have created, based partly on your past experiences, painful or otherwise.

Rather than picking at the wounds of another, why not heal your own wounds? Open to the Truth that everyone is wounded and choose to live life more joyfully. If you are irritated by someone else's actions, use it as the gift it is. Heal you own tender wound.

Reflecting on Mirrors

Only in relationship can you know yourself, not in abstraction and certainly not in isolation.

~ Krishnamurti

∂∽✄

How would our experience of the world be different if it didn't contain mirrors? I get up in the morning and go to the mirror to brush my teeth, to comb my hair, and to see how good or how bad I look.

I have mirrors in my bathroom, bedroom, and living room. The living room mirror adds depth to the room and gives it a sense of a larger space. I find mirrors in public places, such as in hallways and corners, which also add a broader perspective. Who could argue that mirrors serve a useful purpose by providing us with an honest look at ourselves? Are our collars laying flat or is our hair out of place?

The people in our lives who act as mirrors for us are just as useful and important. While the neighbor who remarks on your new haircut gives you a lift, you may just as well get negative feedback. Mirrors do not only show the good about us. They show our reflections: who we really are and how we are seen.

Our most intimate relationships (e.g., spouse, significant other, or boss) also act as mirrors. Since we are around them most often, we show them our most unguarded selves. We may find that what they mirror back is often what we don't like about ourselves.

Regardless of what is being mirrored, I find it useful to consider what my husband reflects back to me. Pondering this feedback with self-honesty opens my mind to new insights and encourages positive change. This is possible because I also know he loves and honors me.

Like a mirror on the wall, intimate relationships can be important if we want to know how we are behaving, what we are expressing, and who we are being in the world.

I have learned to appreciate my husband, my friends, and other personal relationships for their reflection because I know it aids my self-understanding.

Reflect on the mirrors in your life. Are you happy with what they are reflecting? Be grateful for what they show you. You have the power to change what they see.

Learn from the Behavior of Others

Appreciation is a wonderful thing; It makes what is excellent in others belong to us as well.

~ Voltaire

૭જ્જી

If the criteria we use to judge other people's behavior are what our actions would be in a similar situation, guess what? We are doomed to be disappointed.

Since we are all unique individuals with different life experiences, it is unrealistic to judge others using the same criteria we use to determine our own behavior. As a matter of fact, we often hold ourselves to a very high standard. If it is hard for us to live up to our own standards, what makes us think others can do so?

This was brought to mind recently when I heard a friend say, "If I were Susie, I would never have done that. How could she do such a thing?"

My guess is that Susie's actions were based on completely different personal motivations, values, and expectations from those of my friend, which she arrived at through very different life experiences.

When faced with an action that surprises or appalls you, consider what you can learn from the other's action. Rather than judging by using the measure of your own likely behavior, you could gain insight by asking questions.

Ask why they did what they did and then *listen*. Ask what the person was thinking and then *listen*. Open up to the possibility that the measures you use to judge others just might not include the whole picture. At the very least, you may find out what drives people and gain some understanding. However, you may also discover that there is another way to think about a situation and thus change your actions.

By opening up to the possibility that there are other ways to think and act than are in your repertoire, you grow and your world expands.

The next time you find yourself thinking "If I were so-and-so, I'd never do that," expand your world to consider that so-and-so may have something to teach you.

Powerful Words Said in the Moment

The way we see the problem is the problem.

~ Stephen Covey

◈◈◈

While having breakfast one morning, my husband and I were discussing our differences and sharing our thoughts about the issues that had come up between us the day before. Just as all relationships have moments of stress, there are times that my relationship with my beloved Chuck can get intense.

We are both strong-willed, determined people, so it is natural that there are times when conflict arises. Our relationship works because, when we find moments of conflict, we negotiate and resolve them together.

After some very intense, but honest, sharing, the following words came out of his mouth: "The things that I don't like about myself are the very things I don't like about you."

What an amazing moment of awareness! He hit the nail on the head. This, in my opinion, is the basis of most conflict in the world. The very things we do not like about ourselves are what trip us up when we interact with others.

In fact, from my perspective, the way to the much sought-after world peace about which everyone talks begins with finding inner peace and harmony with who we are as individuals. The work of world peace is the work we must each do to know, love, and appreciate who we are in our uniqueness.

That being true, my task (our task) is to become conscious of all the things about others that bother me and turn that awareness back toward myself.

> *What part of this annoyance that I feel for others is an unhealed or unloved part of myself?*

With that insight, I can then do the real work of enlightenment: turn God's Love into self-love and watch the transformations take place in all of my relationships!

The Problem of Unequal Relationships

When you meet someone better than yourself, turn your thoughts to becoming his equal. When you meet someone not as good as you are, look within and examine your own self.

~ Confucius

❧❦

The heart-wrenching news of Iraqi prisoner abuse and torture began surfacing in late 2004. While I have tried not to focus too much on the details, I found the photos and personal accounts appalling, just as you probably did.

As a result, I gained an awareness of the inherent problem of unequal relationships. When one person is perceived as less important or valuable than another, abuses of all kinds can happen.

In fact, unequal relationships harm the powerful as well as the weak. The ego of those who hold power over others takes control and eclipses the goodness of their Soul. Those who perceive themselves as weak become drowned in fear and victimhood, unable to know their own worth.

The U.S. Declaration of Independence proclaims "that all men are created equal, that they are endowed by their Creator with certain unalienable Rights, that among these are Life, Liberty and the pursuit of Happiness. ..."

To be sure, "equal" does not mean "the same," but it does mean that each person is inherently of equal value in the sight of the Creator. Therefore, it is our task to establish a society where each person is in essence equal—of equal importance and worthy of equal respect.

If that's our national intention as codified in the Declaration of Independence, as a nation, isn't this how we should be interacting within the world community?

What does this mean for us personally?

Since any nation is a reflection of its citizens, we are all obliged to scrutinize our personal relationships. How might we be contributing to this inequality?

In what circumstances do you feel more powerful than or less valuable than another? In those relationships, you are in trouble and in danger of being abused or being the abuser.

Consider shifting your perception and your behavior. No one is more valuable than you are; they are just different with different skills and responsibilities. You are not more powerful or more important than others.

Valuing diversity, without making others better or worse than you, will free you to pursue your own happiness!

Maintaining Boundaries, Not Erecting Barriers

When you respect your own "NO!" then others will, too.

~ Rebbetzin Chana Rachel Schusterman

ॐॐ

Having healthy boundaries is frequently discussed as desirable for a well-function person. What is meant by "healthy boundaries"?

Have you ever seen a child at play go over and take a toy out of another child's hand? Young children do not understand what is theirs and what belongs to someone else. However, by the time that child is a teenager, taking a classmate's walkman from his desk is called stealing. We are expected to grow up and learn that there are boundaries between what is ours and what is not.

Having healthy emotional boundaries are also necessary if we are going to mature into healthy, happy people. Our childhood environment should have taught us about emotional as well as physical boundaries. Unfortunately, some of us didn't have good training, possibly because those who raised us never learned about emotional boundaries for themselves.

If you never had the right to your own thoughts (except those in agreement with your parents), your own feelings (and not rejected as silly), or some sense of personal privacy, you may not have developed healthy emotional boundaries.

The result is that some of us go through our adult lives seeking validation from others, never feeling okay with our own efforts. We may take on the feelings of others, always trying to please and soothe them, becoming great at paying attention to everyone else's needs and poor at caring for ourselves.

When I awoke to the fact that I had spent much of my life valuing others above myself, I decided to develop a strong relationship with my own needs. It felt strange, as if I were being self-centered or selfish; perhaps I was for a while.

However, it isn't necessary to build a barrier separating you from others as an overreaction, although that may happen for a time.

By taking on responsibility for others, I had overburdened myself and annoyed and diminished others by being overbearing and overly mothering.

As I maintained my personal boundaries, I began to feel happier. The needy friends I once attracted—the ones who drained me—were replaced with friends who gave to me through our friendship as much as I gave, or more.

You have healthy boundaries when you realize that your happiness and well-being ultimately come from taking care of yourself.

You have healthy boundaries when you do not feel responsible for fixing other people's problems. Healthy boundaries also mean that you do not need to keep people out. You can share and give with ease when you have cared for yourself first.

Balance in Relationships

Problems arise in that one has to find a balance between what people need from you and what you need for yourself.

~ Jessye Norman

Relationships require a balance between a focusing on "me" or "us." Where my attention is placed depends on the circumstances.

In my relationship with Chuck, the polarity between being partnership-focused and independence-seeking is often a challenge.

How do our own needs get attention when we are focused on creating a harmonious relationship? How much can we compromise before we lose our sense of self? In reality, both ends of the "self-versus-other" polarity are important.

In day-to-day living, the balance point is never the same. If my partner is ill, I will naturally be called to give more attention to his needs. When he is well, I may return to balance by taking extra time to pursue my own interests.

In a collaborative relationship, the balance between being alone and being together is a moving target that allows for "a dance of opposites." He will sometimes agree to eat at my favorite restaurant and I will sometimes watch his chosen movie.

Pay attention to the clues to determine how you are doing. How balanced are you feeling within your relationships? Have you been doing all the giving? What can you do or say to bring back the feeling that your needs are also being met and that you are receiving as much as you are giving?

Balancing efforts pay back by recognizing how much you appreciate the relationships you have. Appreciation can blossom when the feeling of balance has been restored by either learning to receive more or by graciously giving more.

All of our relationships (e.g., intimates, colleagues, and friends) can benefit when we pay attention to the balance of giving and receiving. Like the Chinese symbols for balance—yin and yang—we are reminded that we are whole when we are able to balance the giving and receiving in our relationships.

Listening to Those with Whom We Disagree

A person who can embrace others who disagree with them while remaining humble in attitude and inclusive in behavior would create the possibility for peacemaking in the world.

~ Julie Redstone of Light Omega

ॐ ॐ

After the election of President Obama in 2008, I happened to hear a television pundit make a statement about then President-Elect Obama's cabinet selections. Remarking how three of his choices were also fellow presidential candidates during the primary season, the pundit suggested that Obama must be following the adage to "Keep your friends close and your enemies even closer."

Why does someone you once ran against have to be your enemy? To me, it sounded like more of the old separatist thinking that makes an enemy out of everyone with a different viewpoint, even if only slightly different. Disagreement alone does not make an enemy of anyone.

As we move into the Aquarian Age, the norm will be that everyone has important wisdom to share, derived from their unique life experiences. Because we do not all have the same life experiences, each of us has a different point of view. That is a blessing!

Like the adage, "Two heads are better than one," multiple perspectives, shared in an environment that honors all perspectives, will make for a more inclusive society that works for all its members.

The Aquarian ideal of "unity in diversity" means that each individual has value and, when we welcome everyone's contribution, we become a better functioning society.

It is noted that President Obama responded by saying that he intends to listen to his friends but listen even more to those who disagree with him. A person who is humble and wise enough to learn from those with whom he disagrees could break new ground.

Such a president has the potential to lead by example—an example that appeals to the "better angels" of our nature as Americans and as citizens of planet Earth in the 21st century.

Agreeing to Disagree

If you have learned how to disagree without being disagreeable, then you have discovered the secret of getting along—whether it be business, family relations, or life itself.

~ Bernard Meltzer

☙❧

I learned the importance of "agreeing to disagree" from my family, but not the way you might think.

My family had a particular template for behavior and beliefs that I was expected to swallow as a child, even though I have always been naturally self-determined and freedom-loving.

As long as I lived under their roof, I wisely did not rock the boat, at least outwardly. After leaving home, I explored many philosophies and gained diverse life experiences as I matured.

The difference between parental values and my newly gained perspectives erupted into conflict with my folks. I will not trouble you with the details, but let us just say we did not always exchange loving words.

As a result of my many group activities—for learning, for serving, and for fun—I discovered how very diverse people's thinking can be. I found myself in the dilemma of really liking someone but not agreeing with them on some issue.

How could this be? I loved and respected someone—he was my friend—and yet, on some point, we did not see eye to eye. The dissonance was so great that it broke through the old parental mores (you know, the ones that say "you must agree with me because I know what's right").

When the barrier that claimed there is a "right" and "wrong" way to do things fell, I discovered a respectful, peer-to-peer approach that worked much better: "agreeing to disagree." By embracing the idea that two people don't always have to agree, you express respect for the other person *and* yourself.

Ultimately, I learned that I don't need to confirm I am "right" by getting the other's agreement. There are situations where we are both right—right for ourselves and our own life but not right for the other.

Perhaps you have some area of your life where you have been expecting someone to see things your way. What if you accepted that you were both right, or if you simply "agreed to disagree"? Wouldn't it make life more harmonious?

My relationship with my family has greatly improved since I got past expecting them to see my point of view. There are still a few touchy topics we don't discuss, but that leaves more time for sharing what really matters: the love among us.

* * *

In close interpersonal and casual social interactions, the willingness to disagree as well as the acceptance of disagreement needs to be reframed as beneficial. Let me explain.

Have you ever found yourself agreeing with a group decision when inside you were not entirely convinced? It can appear to be so much easier to go along with the majority rather than voice what you are feeling. However, how did you feel afterward?

By not sharing your perspective, several things may have happened. You probably felt uncommitted to the decision and/or were less interested in the group itself. You may not have realized that your failure to offer the group another point of view was disrespectful of the group's purpose. Your perspective might actually have made a difference in the decision.

When we hold back from expressing our viewpoint, we have dismissed ourselves *and* we have withheld something important from others. What do I mean? In a sense, you have failed to provide others with a holistic view of the situation.

I believe that each of us holds a unique perspective—a unique piece—of the holographic world. Without every one of us contributing our piece to the world puzzle, the world remains incomplete.

Therefore, when you are trying to reach a decision within a group, the most holistic thing to do is to share your view, even if it seems in opposition to someone else's ideas. You can do that without being confrontational.

The process of getting all points of view on the table offers more complete information. Reaching a group decision may then be easier; even if it isn't, everyone will be invested in the outcome and all will feel heard when a course of action is finally accepted.

Don't discount your opinion for the sake of harmony. There is definitely an advantage to disagreement. New information has often changed my vote, even when I thought I already knew the right answer.

Inner and Outer Harmony

Happiness is when what you think, what you say, and what you do are in harmony.

~ Mohandas Gandhi

తిం౷ళ

Have you ever found yourself agreeing with someone while inside you knew that you do not agree at all? You may have justified it by thinking you were maintaining peace and harmony with the other person; however, you were really warring with yourself.

When your actions and/or words do not ring true on the inside, you are out of integrity and in conflict with yourself.

The word "integrity" is related to the word "integrate," which means to make whole or unify. When we have integrity, we have harmonized and integrated our outer behavior with our true Inner Self and its values.

It is easy to see how a lack of integrity may have begun. As children, we were disciplined to follow parental norms (often for safety and other good reasons) and avoid our instincts. We may have also learned how to behave according to expectations (at least in front of our parents) while disagreeing with them on the inside. This is the origin of the "shadow," as described by Carl Jung—the realm of rejected instincts and other supposed "bad" parts of us.

However, now that we are adults and, conceivably, know when our outer behaviors are in conflict with our inner values, the path to wholeness lies in paying attention and responding to the need to bring outer behaviors into harmony with our Inner Self. Be aware of when you are not being truthful as you interact in the world.

What is the price of not bringing harmony between our inner values and our outer behavior?

I used to justify my lack of integrity by thinking that I was being nice to others. I would decide whether the other person could handle the truth. I thought it was all about their ability to accept my opinion.

In reality, I was deceiving myself. The true reason I was often out of integrity and misrepresenting my inner truth was because of my fear that others would not accept my truth. I gave them the power to determine whether I was right or wrong, good or bad—just as I had given that same power to my parents as a child.

Now, fortunately, who I am and what I value and believe is no longer negotiable. I have regained authority over my life by establishing my own values and beliefs as the measure of my behavior and no one else's.

I am now free to speak my truth. Sometimes I fall short but, on those occasions when I slip back into pleasing someone else, I don't beat myself up. I just recommit to living from my own inner authority.

As I move through life, the inner and outer harmony of living in integrity by being truthful is a powerful choice. I made this choice on the path to seeking personal wholeness, joy, and fulfillment. It can be powerful for you as well.

Hello! How Are You?

Honesty is the first chapter in the book of wisdom.

~ Thomas Jefferson

❧ ❧

These words of greeting are often exchanged several dozen times a day. Could the fact that they are spoken so frequently be the reason we commonly offer a passive response like "Fine, thank you" or simply brush off answering at all?

I have noticed lately how often I merely say "fine" even when I am actually feeling tired or down. Am I being dishonest? What about simply being cordial? Why dump your troubles on a passer-by?

I agree, in principle, that there are different levels of intimacy and that you may not care to share your troubles with a passer-by, but what about honesty? How do you respond with honesty when you are asked, "How are you?"

The Toltec shaman, Don Miguel Ruiz, in writing about successful living in his book, *The Four Agreements*, identifies the first agreement as "Be impeccable with your word." This means we should speak with integrity, saying only what we mean.

Taking this as my goal, I would say "fine" if I were fine; I would say "tired" if I am tired. If I didn't want to share that I was feeling down, I would be more impeccable if I said nothing.

Clearly, what we say has impact. Our words are not insignificant. Consider that even the offering of a shallow response to a greeting from a passer-by has a result. One result is clouding the possibility of developing a deeper relationship with that person.

By the same token, as you pass someone, do you really want to know how they are? If you don't want a truthful answer (such as "Terrible! I was just diagnosed with cancer."), then perhaps it would be more impeccable to just say "hello."

In fact, how would all our conversations be different if we were mindful of being impeccable with our words?

Opening to Natural Allies

Every friend you have today was once a stranger.

~ Juanita Ruth One

❧❦

One of the deep desires within us is to feel a sense of belonging and being a part of a community. We may feel alienated as we go about our daily lives—never talking to neighbors, carrying on only work-related conversations with office mates, or living far away from our family.

I believe the lack of a sense of community has its origin inside us. Are you suspicious of others when you meet them? Are you worried about what they might want from you? Do you feel insecure and afraid that you have nothing to offer? Our fears and insecurities prevent us from opening to the natural allies who are all around us.

In the past, the fear of not being worthy enough to warrant attention from others, or the fear that they might expect something I was unable to offer, had been my normal response to meeting new people. After years of self-discovery and personal growth, I realized how these behaviors prevented me from the very thing I desired: an open sharing with another and a feeling of belonging.

There are natural allies we meet in everyday life and yet we may pass them by, missing the opportunity to know them. What if you could take the focus off yourself (e.g., how you look, whether you are worthy, or what you fear) and put the focus on others?

Try conversing with the neighbor who never seems to look up. She may be shy and fearful just like you. Say "good morning" and add a comment about something you share (e.g., the neighborhood, the weather, or the tax rate). Ask about some aspect of her life and see what happens. It's possible that you have been missing the opportunity to know someone more deeply and someone you would really enjoy getting to know.

This same approach can be used in the office, at the grocery story, in the doctor's office, or anywhere you go. Make an adventure out of talking to people and finding out about them, as if you were following clues to uncover a mystery. Who are my natural allies? Who around me has shared similar life experiences, enjoys the same music, holds the same beliefs and values, or enjoys the same foods?

Open to your natural allies and you may be astonished at the many people with whom you resonate. At last you will have found the sense of community you were missing!

What Good is Competition?

If we are all one, then which approach serves us better, ultimately, competition or collaboration?

~ W. Scott Erickson

❧ ❧

When I came across this quote from my friend Scott, it took me no time at all to answer it: collaboration, I thought. Posed as a question, it presented me with a great opportunity for deeper consideration.

In many parts of our contemporary life, competition rules in business, sports, and sadly often even in relationships. However, what good *is* competition anyway?

I believe that much of the competition we take for granted is actually born of the false belief that we need to be better, smarter, stronger, or richer than others in order to be important, valued, and praised. Most competition actually works to separate us from others so we can stand above or rule over them.

Those who reach that pinnacle of "the best" often find it lonely and, of course, a difficult place to remain as others naturally challenge anyone on top in a desire to reach the pinnacle themselves.

Collaboration, on the other hand, offers the opportunity to excel in the company of colleagues, to call out the best of others to join your best, thus creating something better than any *one* alone could achieve.

One thing that is needed, however, is to let go of the desire for the spotlight to fall on only you. The ability to enjoy seeing everyone succeed is found in knowing, through the eyes of Oneness, that everyone's success is yours, too.

So what good is competition? I believe the best use of competition is when you are competing with yourself.

Have you done something better today than you did yesterday? Are you sharpening your skills or producing a better product or service? Then you are using competition in the best possible way: to grow and achieve.

What If We Understood Unanimity?

My existence is caught up and inextricably bound up with yours ... A solitary human being is a contradiction in terms.

~ Archbishop Desmond Tutu

෨෬

Our interconnected world is coming vividly into our awareness as the environmental crisis becomes more obvious. Everyone everywhere is affected when the ozone layer thins, when the pH of the ocean acidifies, and when forests are destroyed by the acid rain of industrial smog far away.

The now ubiquitous Internet has also awakened us to how interconnected the world is when, in a matter of seconds, news and rumors can be spread like a virus, infecting or informing even remote villages connected by satellite. However, what are the implications of this interconnectivity? What if we understood unanimity?

The word "unanimity" is derived from the root words "uni" (meaning one) and "anima" (meaning Soul).

If we recognized that we (i.e., humans, planets, animals, *everything*) are part of one interconnected global Soul, how might our lives be different?

+ Our actions would be decided based on the outcome for the others since, if we are connected, our behavior affects, reflects, and influences us as it affects others.
+ Our judgments of others would become judgments of us since, if we are one Soul, our criticisms are ultimately aimed at us.
+ The loneliness and lack of belonging that is felt by many would disappear in the reality that we are parts of one whole.
+ Acts of kindness to others would increase since they would be known to be acts of our own self-love.
+ Polluting or damaging the environment would be unthinkable since part of us would also be harmed.
+ Interpersonal conflicts, wars, and other struggles would be unspeakable as we recognized that listening to others' points of view and negotiating agreements are acts of learning to know ourselves at a deeper level.

- Eating could be seen as a celebration of appreciation for the plants and animals who share their life with us.

There could be many more possibilities for living harmonious, fulfilled, and joyful lives when we understand unanimity with all of Creation. What other thoughts do you have that could add to a vision of a world that worked for *every being?*

All Relationships are Equally Interdependent

… everything and everyone in Life is experienced as being One With You in the moment you accept that you are One With God.

~ Neale Donald Walsh

ॐ ॐ

When Thomas Jefferson wrote the American Declaration of Independence from England in 1776, the words "we hold these truths to be self-evident that all men are created equal" expressed a revolutionary thought. Most people at the time did not find this idea at all self-evident, considering the fact that slavery was flourishing and women were neither given an education nor able to vote.

Today, in the U.S., we are still seeking to demonstrate the promise of the equality of which that document declared. It has been suggested that equality refers to equality of opportunity rather than exact sameness. Could there still be more to learn about what equality means and how we would behave differently if we discovered its greater meaning?

I offer an enhancement to Jefferson's concept that, if understood, could greatly add to its meaning and to our ability to live this truth in our daily lives:

> All relationships are equally interdependent—each one an
> interaction among unique aspects of Creation—and are to
> be treated with fairness, respect, honesty, and compassion.

"All relationships" means every relationship we can imagine (e.g., personal, communal, corporate, national, and international) and some we may not have thought about (e.g., with animals, plants, minerals, and even planets).

At the personal level, with our spouse or significant other, it may be easy to recognize that healthy, intimate relationships naturally include fairness, respect, honesty, and compassion. Examples are plentiful of relationships—perhaps in our own families—that have broken the honesty clause or have missed opportunities for loving compassion; these become models of what does not work in relationships.

Numerous self-help books have made us aware of how to be in intimate relationships that recognize interdependence and encourage the values of fairness, respect, honesty, and compassion.

What about other relationships? What shifts in our behavior when this idea is applied to other relationships beyond our most intimate ones? In our community, applying the standard of fairness, respect, honesty, and compassion would alter how we make zoning decisions, meet the needs of the homeless, and find job opportunities for the unemployed.

Knowing our interdependence, we would recognize that mental health and drug treatment programs are simply necessary for our own personal healthcare gained through living in a healthy community. We would place greater value on their importance. Educational opportunities for everyone would abound.

What about corporations? U.S. law currently views corporations as people and includes such rights as free speech. It may seem strange to apply this to corporate relationships but the same holds true. The relationship between a corporation and its stockholders, its employees, its customers, or the community in which it operates is equally interdependent. Fairness, respect, honesty, and compassion are still applicable in each of these relationships and none is more important than the other.

Currently, stockholders receive the greatest attention, while employee relations and even community relations are simply a necessary but troublesome matter. Imagine how many fewer lawyers would be needed to defend or demand good corporate relationships!

How differently our national governments would function if they worked interdependently. Politics would become an honorable profession reserved for the most ethical among us. Our representatives would still seek the support of those with money and influence and also know that, without exhibiting a sense of fairness, respect, honesty, and compassion to all their constituents, they would have no job.

In theory, that is how things should work now. One reason that doesn't happen is that we fail to see our interdependence with our elected officials. All eligible voters would treasure the opportunity to express their interdependence with their nation by voting in every election and using the measure of fairness, respect, honesty, and compassion to determine their choice. Winning election to public office would become as respected as receiving the Nobel Peace Prize—a sign of high integrity and a commitment to equal interdependence.

Some say we will always have wars and that they are an inevitable part of the human existence. That may be true when humanity operates only through the animal instinct of competition and conquest.

However, under the doctrine of equal interdependence of all nations, there would be no need for conquest or loss of life on either side. If nations began to recognize and practice fairness, respect, honesty, and compassion among them, conflict resolution would look very different.

Differences that naturally occurred would be approached with an expectation of a solution because we would realize that our own best interests—peace and harmony—could best be achieved through negotiation and cooperation. What a magnificent exchange of cultures, ideas, foods, and religious traditions would flourish when all nations knew equally their interdependence with every other nation!

To consider all relationships, we must include those that are not human. The natural world—plants, animals, and Earth herself—is intimately connected to and important for sustaining human existence. Our scientific, mechanistic view of life has resulted in a separation in our relationship to nature, to the point of peril for our children's future.

Our interdependence with nature couldn't be more evident. We depend on plants, through photosynthesis, to produce the very oxygen we breathe, while plants are dependent on our exhaling carbon dioxide to fuel their life, also through photosynthesis. Clearly, we damage ourselves as we wreak havoc on the natural world.

All possible applications of this principle are left to you to consider and discover. This concept, if broadly and sincerely applied, would change the quality of all our relationships. Why not spend some time considering just how this applies to your various relationships? What changes will you make as you recognize interdependence? How can your behavior exhibit more fairness, respect, honesty, and compassion as you relate to all those around you? What if you started today by treating all relationships with the same fairness, respect, honesty, and compassion?

Don't forget your relationship with yourself and how much more quickly you would discover a more loving, peaceful, cooperative world!

Your Soul and God are counting on it.

We need to update the U.S. Declaration of Independence to express a higher understanding of what was created over 200 years ago.

Tom Atlee of The Co-Intelligence Institute has written a Declaration of Interdependence:

> *We hold this truth to be self-evident*
> *We are All In This*
> *Together.*

Therefore we live this truth
in our lives, communities and societies,
and thrive together into a long future
that we create together.

We are the world
that is awakening
to both the fact and the opportunity
of our interdependence—
fully, finally and beyond a shadow of doubt.

We are the world,

Who are making
ourselves a good world
that works for all people and all life.
Because we know the Greatest Secret
of All:

We are All
in this Together.

From Fear to Fraternity

Peace is not won by those who fiercely guard their differences but by those who, with open minds and hearts, seek out connections.

~ Katherine Paterson

৵৵

I can remember the beautiful blue sky on September 11, 2001—the day that airplanes became missiles creating confusion, chaos, and fear.

Like everyone else, I was astounded by what had happened and remained glued to my television set for days. What exactly had happened? How could those buildings fall?

More importantly, *why* had this happened to the U.S.? We were told "They hate our freedoms," but that just did not ring true for me. I felt a need to look from a deeper perspective.

When one part of humanity attacks another part of humanity under any circumstance (e.g., Al Qaida to the U.S., the U.S. to Baghdad, or me to my neighbor), it seems to me that it is because the feelings of alienation and separation have overshadowed the reality that all life is of one essence and that *we are all one.*

If you agree with me—that life is always seeking to move toward more wholeness—then the message of 9/11 was a wake-up call (a 911 call, if you will) to humanity (and to the U.S. in particular) to recognize that we have been acting out of separation from ourselves and our Oneness with others. By this event, we had been given the opportunity to heal and remember our brotherhood with all people.

Sadly, that was not the response that the U.S. government chose and so the separation continues. Instead, we became mired in death and destruction in Afghanistan and Iraq.

On every September 11th, we should choose to remind ourselves to move away from fear and separation and toward awareness of being kindred.

Perhaps you will join me as I hold the vision of a world that celebrates diversity and recognizes our common humanity. I see people of all ages, all ethnicities, all religions and philosophies, and all economic levels living together and discovering each other's unique gifts.

See us honoring our past fear and offering it up to be purified on the fires of transformation. May a new awareness of our inherent brotherhood and fraternity rise from the ashes like a phoenix!

Chapter 4
Surfing the Waves of Change

There is a great deal of difference between loss, change and transformation. A loss is a step backward. A change is an opportunity. Transformation is a step forward.

The common denominator of these three realities is the fact that one must give up something. It is possible for both loss and change to lead to transformation. But it is not possible for transformation to occur unless something is lost and something is changed.

~ Anthony Padavano

When Change Comes

It takes a lot of courage to release the familiar and seemingly secure, to embrace the new. But there is no real security in what is no longer meaningful. There is more security in the adventurous and exciting, for in movement there is life, and in change there is power.

~ Alan Cohen

❧❦

When change comes along, what can you do? You can resist and cling to the old or surrender and go with the flow. One choice involves the stress of trying to hold on to the past; the other involves the stress of an uncertain future.

The first thing to realize is that we all have varying abilities to manage change. Some find change quite disconcerting. Their strength lies in stability and reliability. When their life moves into a period of change, which happens to everyone at some point, it is upsetting. They are likely to resist whatever is happening, at least at first.

Perhaps you've heard the adage, "What you resist, persists." Eventually, everyone must turn over the topsoil of their life. Then, you may find that the fertile soil beneath your habitual existence contains more possibilities for happiness than you ever imagined. When we discover the outcome, we may wonder what we feared and why.

Others have a great ability to go with the flow. Changes come easily, even though they can often be influenced by external circumstances or other people. When changes happen, they may blame others, even though they secretly hoped for them.

Some manage change well as long as they are calling the shots. Being assertive and self-directed, they resist any change that was not invited, but it comes anyway.

Clearly, change is a constant in life. Fortunately, it usually (but not always) comes in cycles that offer a breather between disruptions, allowing time to catch your breath and make adaptations.

One of my clients suffered several major changes over a three- to four-year period, which were tough to handle. Afterward, however, her world was "brand new." Like a clean slate, she created a new life and new growth resulted.

When change comes to call, why not view the unknown as a friend and not something to fear? If fears arise and you want to understand the timing and significance of what is happening, consulting an astrologer may bring clarity.

Waiting to Exhale? Breathe.

Having worked ourselves into a fever over the future of Western civilization,
We will now begin enjoying our oatmeal again
with raisins, chopped apricots and honey
From bees that grazed in meadows of clover.

The beauty of engagement is disengagement.
You simply put on your jacket and walk out the door
And find good health.

There is no fever that a 10-mile hike can't cure
or a donation to charity, or helping a neighbor,
or simply bringing newspapers to the animal shelter,
or visiting someone in a nursing home …
Life goes on, on the most basic of levels.

~ Garrison Keillor

∽∾

As I interact with friends at recent social events, I notice many people acting as if they are shell-shocked. The economic crisis and world events have shaken up our comfort zone and many appear to be "waiting to exhale."

Even folks who have plentiful resources are feeling insecure and cautious. They are hoping that things will settle down soon and go back to normal (whatever that is).

It is clear to me that we are in the midst of a major period of transformation—not only in the U.S., but throughout the world. Our first response when times are uncertain is to retreat. However, retreat is actually a subtle form of denial.

Instead, we need to consider a strategy that is sustainable for the next several years as we are in the process of creating new foundations for our society. The transformations ahead will not happen in a year or even two, thus "waiting to exhale" is not a viable strategy.

If you are waiting to exhale, you might want to start breathing soon or risk falling unconscious from fear. It is true that you are influenced by external circumstances but, if you are reading this book, you are already someone who is conscious and thinks outside the box.

If, out of fear, you stop spending, you will shut off the flow of the universe, which operates on the basis of circulation—giving and receiving. The economic crisis is a result of people motivated by greed who cornered resources into the hands of a few.

Instead of restricting your spending completely, why not start buying locally? Make your purchase count toward sustaining those businesses in your own backyard whose doors you would like to keep open.

The tide is moving toward local commerce and community actions to preserve a thriving standard of living that is not dependent on unsustainable long-distance transportation costs.

Below are some personal strategies for staying balanced under stressful times of change:

+ *Focus on something positive*, like loving friends, loyal pets, and kind neighbors.
+ *Remember the bounty you have* in your life right now (don't worry about an unknown future).
+ *Disregard the negative energy coming from the media* (perhaps turn off the television or put down the paper).
+ *Laugh* at the absurdities of life and then laugh some more.
+ *Don't isolate yourself;* instead create a community and gather with others whom you enjoy.
+ Be sure to *get a good night's sleep* (everything is easier when you are rested).
+ *Enjoy an inspirational book, a poem, or a song every day.*
+ *Meditate* and feel the inner peace that nothing outside you can disturb.
+ *Cherish this day* and make *every* day one full of appreciation.

Most of all, remember to keep breathing and finding the beauty in every moment.

Being True to Yourself Amidst Outer Confusion

This above all: to thine ownself be true, and it must follow, as the night the day, thou canst not then be false to any man.

~ William Shakespeare, *Macbeth*

ॐ ॐ

Have you been feeling confusion and the awareness of chaos in the external world? This is aided by the news headlines with such topics as mudslinging electioneering, the nuclear saber rattling, the intractable problems of Iraq and Afghanistan, environmental degradation, oil dependence, healthcare cost inflation ... and on and on. These issues, and more, are in your face in the daily newspaper, on television, and on the radio.

Perhaps the confusion may be due to issues that hit closer to home. You may be dealing with job loss or a lack of job satisfaction, an unhappy relationship, or the feeling that something in your life isn't quite right. The issue may leave you feeling lethargic, unfocused, and uncertain as to what to do about it. What *is* a person to do?

Through all the outer confusion, it is imperative that you are true to yourself by honoring your own needs while being bombarded by the needs of others. The truth is that I am so much better at honoring and supporting others than I am at honoring myself.

Were you taught that it is better to give than receive? Now that is a prescription for burnout if I ever heard one! When you give without receiving, you end up with nothing left to give. That is certainly *not* in harmony with the flow of life. To prove it, try only breathing *out*.

Being true to yourself requires that you open up to receive from others or from life in whatever way grace shows up. Being receptive does not mean searching or seeking to receive; it means merely holding open the possibility that life has something to give you without your having to do anything but maintain faith and express gratitude.

In addition, honoring yourself requires being honest. In the act of being a good giver, have you ever discovered that you compromised or accommodated for another person, leaving them thinking that you agreed with them when, in reality, you actually just sublimated your own needs to theirs? You may not have recognized that behavior as being dishonest, but it is.

Focusing only on agreement and avoiding differences is certain to leave your relationship weak, shallow, and dishonest. When you lie to yourself, you end up being dishonest to others as well.

Above all, being true to yourself calls for deeply listening to your inner voice. What does your heart tell you? Take time to meditate, walk in the woods, or just sit and ponder to find greater self-awareness.

Listen to your hopes and dreams as well as your disappointments and dissatisfactions. Hold yourself in a loving way and your next steps will become clear.

Trust the Rhythms of Your Life

Rhythm is the basis of life, not steady forward progress. The forces of creation, destruction, and preservation have a whirling, dynamic interaction.

~ From *Kabbalah*

❧ ❧

Life sometimes feels like a stroll in the park on a sunny day; other times, it's like running a marathon in a pack of thousands. One day may flow easily with a sense of accomplishment, while the next day you awaken out of sorts, unable to perk up.

My life often looks more like a marathon. If I have not written for a while, I may feel guilty that I am not keeping the schedule I set for myself. However, rather than beat myself up, I decided to find out what would happen if I simply trusted myself and the rhythms of my life. Instead of pushing the river of life, I allowed my inner urgings to tell me when to write and when not to, allowing my writing to flow more easily.

When I worked in the corporate world, I would expect myself to be productive from 8am to 5pm every day, as if productivity could happen on schedule, like a mechanized production line. In truth, it is unnatural for me and, I suspect, for most people to schedule accomplishments. Some days I accomplished much; other days, I goofed off. On unproductive days, I felt guilty and nagged myself to do better, promising myself to achieve more the next day.

What if you trusted the rhythms of your life? What if you let your inner urging direct your day? Listening to your inner urge—call it guidance, Soul direction, or inspiration—can result in more achievements and less stress because you would be moving with and not against your natural rhythms.

Of course, deadlines may dictate what you must do and when but, if you look clearly at the present circumstance, you probably still have more flexibility to go with your natural flow than you have been allowing yourself.

The deadlines that are often most stressful are actually the deadlines that are self-imposed. Is your daily "to-do" list so long that no one could finish it, making you discouraged before you begin?

Learning to listen to inner guidance about what to do today allows your day to flow with ease. Take a risk and try trusting what you feel. Trust the rhythms of your life. You'll see how much easier and more joyful life can be!

The Cycles of Life (Darkness and Light)

If we had no winter, the spring would not be so pleasant. If we did not sometime taste adversity, prosperity would not be so welcome.

~ Ann Bradstreet

☜☞

I always relish the sight of the big, bold, Full Moon, drenched in the Sun's light. Its brightness makes even the darkness of night come alive, throwing fairy dust on the objects it touches.

The New Moon, on the other hand, allows so little light that the darkness seems deeper and more mysterious, perhaps a bit ominous at times. Every 29 days, 12 hours, and 44 minutes, this cycle—New Moon to Full Moon and back—has repeated for eons unknown, so naturally we may not have stopped to think of its implication.

If the giver of life (the Sun) and the receiver or embodiment of life (the Moon) follow a modulating cycle of darkness and light, it is only natural that our own lives will follow.

There are times when everything seems to work like a charm, things get done effortlessly, relationships are harmonious, and we're at peace with ourselves. Then there are those other moments when nothing clicks, we feel frustrated at every turn, and life doesn't seem worth the effort. Enter depression and despair.

When I give in to the cycle of the moment, knowing that it will not last, I am rewarded with more contentment no matter what is happening at the time. In actual practice, how does this look?

If everything is abundant and exciting, I remember to be thankful for the moment. Rather than fearing it will end, I acknowledge that this cycle will eventually move into a less productive time and make the best of the moment.

By the same token, at those times when I feel withdrawn, confused, or in despair, I also remember that "this too will pass." Rather than resist, I relax and wait, knowing that this is only a cycle that will transition eventually into a happier, more productive time.

What cycle are you in? Are you making the best of it? Appreciate every cycle of your life. All of life has meaning, whether it is a time of darkness or of light.

Darkness Can Be Preparation for New Growth

When it is dark enough, you can see the stars.

~ Ralph Waldo Emerson

❧◦❧

Every year at the Winter Solstice in the northern hemisphere, daylight is shorter, it is darker longer, and nature hibernates until spring. We refer to this time as "the dead of winter."

Though nothing appears alive, the seeds that will manifest as flowers in spring are inwardly preparing for new growth. Things appear to be inactive even while there is a powerful process underway that will eventually produce new plant life and new beauty.

Such is also the reality of human life, though we may not recognize the connection. Can you remember a time when you felt eager for a change—perhaps a new job or a new relationship—yet nothing in the outer world seemed to be happening? Long periods of time can pass without change. At times like this, we have the opportunity to shift our inner reality.

In order to manifest new possibilities, it may be necessary to shift our inner awareness to match that which we desire. When I yearned for a new relationship, the many months spent on visualizing myself as lovable and capable of maintaining a supportive, loving relationship set in motion the process that ended in meeting my beloved husband.

If you feel stuck and frustrated because your dreams are not becoming a reality, consider what is or isn't happening in your inner reality to support your desired outcome. Are you changing your inner reality to welcome the eventual reality desired?

Those who understand the Law of Attraction know that *your thoughts and feelings create your reality.* Seeing yourself in your mind's eye, enjoying the new life you desire, helps to make it happen. When nothing is happening in your outer existence, recognize that you are being given an opportunity to go within to envision, create, and get excited about the dream you are holding.

Astrology can describe various cycles: times of limitation when, for example, you may be forced to reevaluate your goals and make tangible plans for action, or times when you feel lost in space.

What astrology cannot tell is *what you will choose to do* while you are waiting for the external world to manifest your desire. You can allow yourself to feel frustrated, a victim of dissatisfaction, or you can proactively contribute to creating your desire by feeling and imagining as if it has already happened. What will you choose to do?

Loving and Letting Go

When you discover you are riding a dead horse, the best strategy is to dismount.

~ Dakota saying

❧ ❧

There is a natural process in life that involves letting go. As there cannot be an "in" breath without having just breathed "out," life itself does not complete its process or its expression until it lets go.

However, often we resist the "letting-go" part. How long may we hold on to the past before holding on becomes a deadening action on one's own potential and future? Some people, I notice, let themselves deteriorate by holding on to the memories of the past. Change is harder for some than others, it is true, but there is no denying it as an integral, necessary process of life.

Look at the natural world. There is really no way to keep life from bringing the change called "winter." We harvest the crops and then let go, only to discover new growth in the spring. It would be foolish to try to hold on to the tomato plant. We could shield it from the cold and snow, but it would still die. Our actions would be futile and a waste of time. Nature knows that what grows must die and that new growth will come.

How then can we approach the many circumstances in our lives when we face a time of letting go? I suggest that, by loving, we are able to let go easily and with grace, knowing there will be new growth somewhere in our lives as a result.

If, for example, dear friends announce a move hundreds of miles away, it is your love of them and happiness for their great new job that eases the loss of their presence in your everyday life. Likewise, when your child leaves for college, you can celebrate the event rather than mourn their departure by recognizing, with love, this important step in their maturity.

When my sister died, it was my love for her and my belief that she was now much better off (having left the physical suffering she endured for years) that allowed me to let go of her sweet, loving presence in my earthly life.

Loving and letting go can also be applied to numerous other

situations. I belong to an organization that has been very influential in my growth. The charismatic leader of the organization passed away and, for several years, the energy of the group had been primarily focused on the past. Little or no new life or growth had occurred, only gatherings that focused mostly on the past activities and how significant the leader had been in our lives.

Reminiscence is a good thing if it is part of loving and letting go, but it is a deterrent to growth if it is an expression of holding on to the past and denying change. In actuality, from that organization grew many new projects and initiatives spawned by people influenced by the deceased leader. New possibilities are there for every member when they let go and move on.

Perhaps the best that we can do when we face a situation or circumstance that calls us to let go is to deeply ponder the love that is there. Recognizing the love that was present, we can find peace in letting go and muster the ability to create new possibilities. We can let go of the past by loving it, because love never dies—even though the person, the organization, or the situation will surely end some day.

Shake Up Routines with a Vacation

I travel a lot; I hate having my life disrupted by routine.

~ Caskie Stinnett

આ૦ન૬

Do you feel like you are stuck in a rut? Has daily life become lifeless and too much the same? If you are feeling the call to adventure and change, there is nothing like a vacation to change things.

In fact, it may be the very thing to breathe new life into your existence. Returning home after unusual and interesting experiences, you could bring new ideas about changes you would like to make to your daily routines.

Recently, my husband and I returned from a lovely driving tour of Maine and the maritime provinces of Canada. Moving back into the rhythms of my daily life, I realize that I have the option to change whatever I had done before.

Rather than mindlessly diving into some old behaviors, I could establish an entirely new norm. Why not take a walk or meditate before I even enter my office?

A vacation is an excellent opportunity to scramble your well-trodden life path, open up new vistas and possibilities, and offer a fresh perspective to your life. Perhaps that is why it is well known that a vacation can revitalize your attitude about your life. Do you need a revitalization plan?

Let me add my encouragement. Do not let many months pass before you undertake at least one long weekend when you can venture out of the ruts and explore unknown places, gain new experiences, and share ideas with someone new.

Wherever You Go, There You Are

No matter where you go, there you are.

~ From *The Adventures of Buckaroo Banzai Across the 8th Dimension*, a 1984 movie

ॐ ॐ

Wherever you go, there you are! These words had been rumbling around in my head, though I know I never saw the movie that spawned them. I was feeling uncomfortable with my life the way it was. Perhaps it would be better if we moved someplace else, I thought.

The problem is that wherever we go, we have to take ourselves with us! The reality that I disliked, that I had been arguing with *here*, would just be replaced by someone or something else to argue with when I got *there*, wherever *there* is.

For example, I made a major move from New Jersey to Texas in 1978 and from Texas to Virginia in 1986. Each time, I was eager to throw my life into the chaos of a move because there were issues I wanted to escape.

Of course, if you really change internally as well as externally, the new location will prove to present a fresh, new start. However, if you don't also change internally, you'll just find the same problems looking at you through different eyes.

Each of my moves, in fact, did nothing to solve the problems I wanted to leave behind. Fortunately, I finally woke up. I have not moved since. That does not mean I would not choose to move again in my life, but it will not be because I want to run away from anything.

Finally, I have learned that, if I want to change my life, I need to change myself, my beliefs, and my behaviors. Real outward change happens then, often magically.

As another example, I had a boss who was very critical and confrontational. I loved my work but found the office environment toxic. Every night when I went home, I felt drained. Then, I was introduced to the idea that I played a part in creating the situation by my own attitude. Upon reflection, I realized I had also been critical of *her*.

As an experiment, I decided to go to the park every day during lunch and spend time visualizing the two of us having a friendly conversation. In my imagination, I thanked her for her helpful support and heard her say that I was doing a good job. Magically, within a week, the relationship began to improve. A few months later, when I left the job (for a different reason), she was the one who expressed the greatest sadness to see me leave.

Wherever you go in your life, remember that your own inner attitude and beliefs create your world. Want to change your circumstances? *Change your attitude and beliefs*. It is much easier and less expensive than moving across the country only to learn that ... *oops!* There you still are!

Politics Versus Spirituality

Spiritual forces are moving deeply and powerfully behind the scenes of world events in ways that are not obvious on the evening news. Today's headlines, viewed with the right consciousness, can be seen as a living alphabet through which humanity comes to know itself and God. A deeper meaning is revealed.

~ Corinne McLaughlin,
Spiritual Politics: Changing the World from the Inside Out

಄ೀ

Politics is rather unspiritual, right? After all, it is often nothing more than dirty power mongering—the playground of power and privilege. If I am spiritually inclined, why would I want to get involved in such matters?

Like many of the Watergate generation, I have complained bitterly about the political process and its unsavory results or lack thereof. In the next breath, I may slyly repeat the joke about "two things that you don't want to see being made: sausage and legislation."

It is easy to discount our ability to make a difference in the process. Does our vote count for anything? The freedoms promised in our founding documents require an informed and involved citizenry in order to ensure that those freedoms remain. Have we been shirking our responsibility as citizens of this great nation?

Do you agree with the actions of your government (e.g., foreign policy, economic policy, ecological policy, and policies regarding privacy, education and healthcare)? If not, it is important to make your views known to your congressperson.

No, politics is not intrinsically unspiritual. Believing God to be everywhere present, the qualities of truthfulness, integrity, fairness, and the good of the Whole should be the guiding principles of our political scene. Are they?

It is time for us, who are spiritually focused, to engage and learn about the issues, to consider our values, to speak out, and to take a stand for the kind of government we want, and for how we want to live together in our communities – our nation and the community of nations in the world.

When we advance the highest quality of democracy, and promote the values of truthfulness, fairness, and community, we may actually spiritualize the political process. Politics then can become the expression of Spirit on Earth.

Chapter 5

Creating on Purpose

This is the true joy in life, the being used for a purpose recognized by yourself as a mighty one; the being thoroughly worn out before you are thrown on the scrap heap; the being a force of nature instead of a feverish selfish little clod of ailments and grievances complaining that the world will not devote itself to making you happy.

~ George Bernard Shaw, playwright

Attention! Your Life is Being Created

Thoughts are like data programmed into a computer, registered on the screen of your life. If you don't like what you see on the screen, there's no point going up to the screen and trying to erase it. Thought is Cause; experience is Effect. If you don't like the effects in your life, you have to change the nature of your thinking.

~ Marianne Williamson

❧ ❧

No one can deny that we are living in the age of information; in fact, too much information. We are barraged by television, radio, the Internet, and billboards—you name it. All are seeking to direct our thinking and our choices. From the most effective pain reliever to the current political policy, we are flooded with news, views, ideas, and supposed cures for the "human condition."

Do you realize what is being squandered while you are flooded with all this information? The thoughts on which you put your attention are critically important because *your thoughts create your world*. In fact, what you focus on enlarges and becomes more real.

Even quantum physics is proving that matter is not fixed and the observer affects what is observed. Therefore, in a very real sense, you are creating your life through your focus and attention. In this way, you are always creating your life, consciously or unconsciously.

With that understanding, it becomes very important that we recognize the power we have to create our world. When we choose to put our attention on something, it becomes a powerful tool for self-improvement.

The kinds of movies you watch, for example, are not insignificant. You may say, "That's just entertainment." However, your psyche subconsciously reacts to everything you see as if it were real, even when it isn't. When you get to the scariest parts, don't you jump? Your body imagines that you are being threatened and reacts.

Do you desire more love in your life? Do you yearn for a more peaceful existence? You can create more love and more peace by consciously choosing different places on which to focus your attention.

Begin by removing negativity from your thoughts. What makes you angry, fearful, or hurt? Consider removing the things, activities, and people from your environment who illicit these emotions. We were meant to find joy and love in life, not just pain and suffering. You can take steps in that direction today.

In the words of a Unity church song, "Our thoughts are prayers and we are always praying ... Take charge of what you're saying ..."

May you find more joy and love through thinking (praying) consciously and giving your attention to uplifting subjects. Leave behind what drags you down.

The Importance of Vision

Where there is no vision, the people perish.

~ Proverbs 29:18

The value of living in the moment notwithstanding, it is also true that the very essence of life draws us to look forward toward each succeeding moment. The Bible reminds us that, without the ability to envision the future, we may perish.

By "vision," I mean the ability to image and anticipate a desirable future—one that encourages us to live in the possibility of something higher and better than in the past.

Sometimes we may be called upon to hold a vision for someone who may be depressed and feeling despair. When my sister was very ill, I rushed to the hospital to be with her. When I arrived, she was uncomfortable and despondent. While doing everything I could to make her more comfortable, I noticed that, when I spoke about what was happening in my life and opportunities for the future, she lost the focus on her troubles.

A moment later, her physician arrived with the good news that she would soon be moved out of intensive care. His last comment was, "I want you to start thinking about going home." The doctor and I were holding a positive vision for her when she was having trouble holding such a vision for herself.

It is remarkable how loving words that paint an optimistic future can help others when they are too weak to see anything but the cloud hanging over their head at the moment. We can bring hope of a better future, when others cannot do it for themselves.

Good leaders offer this gift when they express hope for the future. For example, teachers can inspire their pupils to learn and grow, successful managers can encourage their subordinates to develop new skills, and our national leaders could inspire us to come together as a nation to address societal challenges—but not all do.

What vision do you hold today? Is there someone in your life who needs you to share your encouraging vision? When you envision the future, you co-create it with God. Your vision can help to create hope for others.

What is Your Apollo 11 Experience?

Whatever you can do or dream you can, begin it. Boldness has genius, power and magic in it!

~ Goethe

❧ ❧

During the 40th anniversary of one of man's paradigm-breaking feats—when man first walked on the moon in July 21, 1969—I reminisced about that moment. Watching the television as Neil Armstrong took his step, I was nursing my first born, Erica, who was a mere three weeks old.

What an incredible accomplishment for man to walk on the Moon! President Kennedy's visionary commitment to land a man on the moon had been a success. It seemed to prove that there are no limits to what is possible if only you set your mind (and commit your resources) to it.

Perhaps landing a man on the moon was not absolutely necessary. Despite naysayers, we undoubtedly benefited from the inventions and discoveries that made it possible. More than that, by this achievement, mankind gained a greater awareness of the universe in which we live and the glory of dreams fulfilled. In fact, the photo of Earth looking back from the moon produced a whole new vision of a single planet—evidence of our Oneness on Earth.

Using the Moon landing as a metaphor, I ask myself, "When have I stretched to commit to something that at the time seemed unattainable?" I did just that when I studied and passed my astrological certification. Indeed, I am doing it again as I write and publish this book.

With any achievement, it was necessary to focus and direct my energies toward one goal. I could not allow distractions. I cancelled subscriptions to prevent being tempted to waste time reading magazines, and declined all but the most essential social invitations. It required intense focus and dedication to my goal to produce success.

What is your Apollo 11 experience? Surely there are new dreams, new goals, and new focuses calling for your attention. Will you commit to them or just drift from day to day? It is your choice!

There is More to *The Secret*

Find thoughts that feel good, because it is inevitable that you are going to always be moving toward something. So why not be moving toward something that is pleasing? You can't cease to vibrate, and the Law of Attraction will not stop responding to the vibration that you are offering.

~ Abraham Hicks

❧❧

The movie and book *The Secret* has gotten lots of publicity lately. Perhaps you learned about in on *Oprah* or from Larry King. Everywhere I turn, someone is talking about it. I confess that I am amazed at its popularity. Obviously, it is an idea whose time has come.

Knowledge and use of the Law of Attraction is a powerful aid in creating the life you wish to live, but is it that simple and does it always work? Have you tried to manifest your dream and gotten discouraged?

There are three principles that I believe are vitally important to understand the Law of Attraction. Without knowing these, you could become disillusioned and revert to negative thinking.

1. **You have to love everything in the present moment while feeling appreciation and gratitude.**

   It is wonderful to design an ideal life, which includes the best job, house, car, and relationship, but the Law of Attraction does not work if you are trying to run away from the moment by dreaming of a better life in the future. Your thoughts of misery will only bring you more misery. You have to find and appreciate what is good in the present moment. That is where the power to create a better next moment is found. Out of gratitude, more will be given.

   My understanding of this came while working in a corporate job that I hated. I sent out dozens of resumes and got one interview for a worse job than the one I had. After spinning my wheels, I decided to relax and remain where I was until the urge to leave due to unhappiness was transformed into the urge to go toward what I would enjoy. I had no clue what I wanted. I only wanted to run away from where I was.

   I ultimately left corporate life to start my astrology practice—the work I thoroughly enjoy—but that didn't happen until I deepened my appreciation for the good parts of the job I had.

2. You have to put your desires into action.

It isn't enough to dream dreams and hope to have them land in your lap. If you really believe in your dreams, you must take strategic steps to manifest them. Often, it starts with the power of the words. You speak of your plans and then you back up your words with action. This is different from trying to make things happen out of an attempt to manipulate a specific outcome. It is more like doing your part in creating the environment from which your desires can appear.

For example, for a long time I had the desire to write a book. I talked about it for a couple years, but I did not even have a working title. It was more or less a vague desire urged from within me. I created a blog so I would be encouraged to write more often. Finally, I just happened to meet a book coach who challenged me to take determined steps by clearing my schedule and taking action, at least by putting some words to paper every day. Right now you are reading the result of following this principle.

3. We do not have ultimate control of the outcome and timing is not in our hands.

The truth of this statement has been proven to me time and again as an astrologer. I can see in a client's chart whether or not the year ahead holds possibilities for manifesting a particular desire.

As all of life has cycles, like breathing in and breathing out, so it is that, just because you desire something, it does not mean you are currently in a cycle of manifesting it. You could be in a cycle of letting go. The Law of Attraction is about "co-creating" with God. From a higher wisdom, what we desire may not yet be right for us now ... or at all. We must sometimes hold the vision and keep the environment open for the manifestation of our dreams for an extended period of time before the timing is right.

At one time, I had a vision and strong yearning for a supportive partner. It took a longer time than I hoped. However, the timing of Chuck Adams entering my life was perfect. We both acknowledge that we were not ready to appreciate the gift of a loving relationship one moment before we actually found each other. I guess I had to kiss a few frogs first before I recognized the Prince!

We create our lives one thought, one moment at a time. Don't let your expectations of mansions and a Mercedes leave you frustrated and disillusioned. You can find a love-filled, abundant, and fulfilling life by living in harmony with the present moment. You can act to create an environment into which your dreams can grow by acknowledging that timing depends on the cycle of receiving and letting go. I call it the "Divine Dance of Life."

Opening Life's Flow with Gratitude

Be thankful and filled with awe and appreciation even if what you desire hasn't yet arrived. Even the darkest days of your life are to be looked on with gratitude. Everything coming from Source is on purpose.

~ Wayne Dyer, *The Power of Intention*

❦

Have you ever noticed how easy it is to focus on what is missing or not quite right in life? Much of my life had been spent focusing on what wasn't there: not enough money, not enough friends, and not enough time. You name it! All that was good was disregarded while I focused on the bad.

Then I discovered the magic of gratitude. By opening my view to encompass all that *is* in my life, it became apparent that all the while my life had been a wonderful stream of people and activities, each offering me a little more happiness, more abundance, and more possibilities.

How does that work? Since thoughts create, my thoughts of "not enough" continued to produce just that, and I continued to find areas of my life that fell short of my expectations. I perpetuated my own unhappiness.

By the same token, when I realized the power of thoughts to create, I experimented with consciously seeking to notice all that was good in my life while feeling thankful and expressing gratitude for what I found. Guess what? More good showed up! I found even more reasons to be thankful!

Here's a simple exercise that will increase the flow of good in your life: Every evening, as you are about to fall asleep, review the activities of your day with a focus on gratitude for all the good that has happened. Don't take for granted the little things. Include them as well. Then observe how your world changes.

If you really want to boost the love in your relationship, sit down with your beloved and share the things for which you are grateful in the other person. It can positively recharge a relationship that has fallen into a rut. Try it!

Remember *what you focus on expands*. Focus on gratitude for all that you have and you will be flooded with more. Happy Thanksgiving all year long!

Expectations Versus Intentions

To the extent we can live without demanding or expecting (except from ourselves), so can we be free from disillusionment and disappointment. To expect something from another because it's right is to court unhappiness. Others can and will only give what they are able, not what you desire they give. When you cease placing conditions on your love, you have taken a giant step toward learning to love.

~ Leo Buscaglia

ᔐ ᔑ

Interest in conscious creation of our reality or "being conscious when interacting with reality" is clearly an important step toward living a life of joy and fulfillment.

When we do this, through what sort of lens are we looking when we focus on our lives? That lens is created by our expectations or intentions. What is the difference?

Expectations, in my view, are what we set up when we create a picture in our mind of what we want. That picture is usually very detailed and specific. Once created, it remains as the template against which we measure anything that appears.

For several years while single, I held a picture of the partner I expected to find. The trouble was that my picture was so idealistic, so perfect, that no one ever matched it. My expectations actually prevented me from finding someone because I was so hung up on the details (e.g., looks and status).

Expectations have a quality of "I want this" and set up anticipation of fulfillment from a self-centered, needy perspective.

On the other hand, intentions arise out of an inner desire or plan for our lives that involves some sort of action. There is willingness to take action to create an appropriate environment out of which what we desire can arise.

For example, when a farmer intends to have a plentiful harvest of crops, he takes the action of planting seeds in spring and weeding regularly through the summer to create the conditions for the fall harvest. If he just sat on his porch, picturing in his mind the way he expects the field to look in the fall, there would be nothing to harvest.

I am describing the difference between wishful thinking and co-creating with our Source. Perhaps that is what is behind the saying, "God helps those who help themselves." The problem of trying to manifest through expectations is that it leaves no room for *something better*.

Going back to my example of having expectations of what my partner would be like, I can tell you that my beloved husband, Chuck, didn't show up until I let go of knowing exactly what was best for me. He has many of the qualities I was seeking but there were many other qualities that I hadn't even factored in and he came in a quite different package than I had "expected."

Basically, when we seek to create the future by definite expectations, we are doomed to disappointment either by not finding anything that could possibly measure up or by finding a match and discovering later that it wasn't quite what we wanted after all.

We can best create success in the future by holding an intention of what we would like. This should include a willingness to create the environment for our desire to appear and an openness to accept our intention of *something better*, leaving room for the universe to gift us beyond our imagination.

This process, creating through intention, is in harmony with the Divine!

* * *

In his book, *The Power of Intention*, Wayne Dyer lays out a 10-step process for manifesting intentions. The last of his 10 steps is to "develop an attitude of gratitude for all that manifests into your life."

For me, an attitude of gratitude is the key difference between "intentions"'" and "expectations."

There was a time when I was full of hopes and wishes. My life at that time was sadly far from what I hoped possible. I would look around at others' lives and wonder why I wasn't getting my dreams fulfilled.

In retrospect, I know that my focus was only on what *wasn't* there; what was missing or unsatisfactory got all my attention. My expectations were not manifesting because I had not learned the importance of being thankful for what already is in my life.

If we aren't grateful for what we have, we are unlikely to be open for something more. We would just be disappointed that it wasn't "the moon and the stars"!

When we hold expectations that come from what we think we

deserve or think is best for ourselves, we could be setting our sights too low or too high. Either way, our concrete picture of desired results is likely to eclipse what turns out to be best for us.

I now prefer to create an intention for my future, take steps to create a welcoming environment in which it can appear, and then give thanks for whatever shows up. I know that whatever shows up is always just right. How do I know that? By looking back and realizing the thread of good that has always been weaving through my life circumstances.

My life is full of more joy, abundance, and fulfillment than I ever imagined. I have a loving partner and a family, highly conscious friends and clients, and opportunities galore to do the kind of work that makes my heart sing while helping others.

The important difference between intention and expectation is *gratitude*.

You can apply my suggestion to the future of your country as well. Help fulfill your hopes for your country by taking the same steps: create an intention, participate in creating the environment that could manifest that dream, and then be grateful for what shows up.

It is important to recognize that the intention process applies in every area of your life.

Observe and Choose, Do Not React

The only devils in the world are those running around in our own heart—
That is where the battle should be fought.

~ Mohandas Gandhi

భా~ఆ

One of the benefits of meditation is the growing awareness of "the Observer" within ourselves. The Observer is the part of us that watches what we do as we do it. It is not our intellect or mind; it comes from another place, which some call the Higher Self or Soul.

Have you ever noticed that, while you were thinking, your thoughts were sometimes self-critical? Perhaps you looked in the mirror and a judgmental thought arose like, "I look terrible! I need to lose some weight." That is just the voice of your ego; the neutral part of you that notices your thoughts and behavior, the Observer, is your higher consciousness or Soul.

As you develop this ability to observe, you will discover that you have a greater ability to manage your life through the power of choice. When something happens, you are less likely to react defensively, self-protectively, or unconsciously. With the Observer awakened, you can step back from the incident and decide what action, if any, would be appropriate that could lead to a positive outcome.

Just a few extra seconds of observation of the situation before responding can make the difference between continued chaos and conflict and the opportunity to create and foster peace and well-being.

Living as I do in the Washington, D.C. area, with its nerve-wracking traffic, a good example is when I am cut off by an aggressive driver. In the past, I would get angry; afterwards, I would feel frustration, annoyance, and even bodily discomfort (e.g., acidic stomach).

As my Observer has gotten stronger, I realize that, when I observe an aggressive act, I can choose to act differently. Rather than let anger arise, I can choose peace—a basic teaching from *A Course in Miracles*.

Although applicable for managing traffic snarls, this same principle can be applied to any situation in your life. You will find that the act of observing the situation helps remove you from its effects. You stop viewing the circumstance as something aimed at you personally. From that place, you are better able to discover more options for responding.

Greater power comes from the ability to choose rather than react automatically (or emotionally).

You can discover new choices by observing, not just reacting to circumstances!

Life is a Matter of Timing

The one who forces time is forced back by time, but the one who yields to time finds time standing at one's side.

~ Babylonian *Talmud*

❧ ❦

As much as I wish it were different, I have come to realize that life is a matter of timing.

Have you ever had a desire you hoped would manifest immediately? As you wish, hope, and worry, nothing happens. As you wait for something to change, you begin to think that you were crazy to think you could ever get your wish fulfilled in the first place.

You may think, "I must not be worthy of it." Disappointed, you make the decision that it was never meant to be and give up, defeated by your inability to make it happen as soon as you had hoped.

This has happened to me time and again. As I have mentioned before, unhappy in my corporate job, I wanted a new position. I cleaned up and enhanced my resume. I researched all the openings in my area of interest and sent out dozens of resumes.

Nothing happened except one unpromising interview. This went on for quite a while until I gave up hope. I began to notice what I *did* like about where I worked. You might say I surrendered to what was my current reality.

The story doesn't end there. In retrospect, I am able to see that the timing was not right for me to take the next step in my life. I was looking for another job, but God had other plans.

My next step, it turned out, was to be self-employed as an astrological consultant. First, however, my entrepreneurial abilities and self-confidence needed to be enhanced before it was possible for the grand opportunity to take my next step could appear.

The whole experience has helped me to see that "right timing" is essential to success. Would it surprise you to know that it took seven years to complete the manifestation of my dreamed-of new direction?

For me, there was work to be done to lay the foundation. Had I avoided the learning and preparation, I would not be as successful and satisfied as I am now—living my passion as an astrologer and writer.

Astrology is an excellent indicator of "right timing." It can quite accurately reveal your current cycle, when it will end, and when a new cycle will begin.

If you are feeling frustrated by a desire that you just can't seem to manifest, it may be that you are not yet at the point of optimal timing. Don't lose heart; fulfillment and satisfaction may yet be ahead.

Unblock and Flow: from First to Third Person

We must learn to hear the tongue of the Invisible.

~ *Qur'an*

ॐॐ

Have you ever been in the midst of an important project and found that your progress was blocked, you were going nowhere, and you just could not muster the energy or find the creative juice to complete it?

Whether it is something creative, like writing an article, or something you want to accomplish, like building a bookcase, there are times when the task ahead can seem to require a Herculean effort.

No one likes feeling blocked but sometimes it happens. You could try pushing yourself, but you would feel like you were walking through molasses. At moments like these, try listening to what your inner voice is saying.

My inner voice often says something like, "If you don't get this right, and get it done soon, you are going to look bad or you are going to let someone down or embarrass yourself."

If your inner voice is worried about how you will look to others, it may be that your ego is too strongly involved in designing the desired result. That is a sure prescription for a muddled outcome or no progress at all.

The best way to return to feeling at ease and moving forward is to shift your perspective from the first person ("How will I look?" and "What should I do?") to the third person ("Who will benefit?" and "What purpose is this serving?").

Rather than focus on how to save face or look good to others—the ego's focus—shift your thoughts to the purpose the project serves. This focus deadens the ego's critical voice and opens the flow of energy toward purpose and service. Is it really necessary to do something perfectly? Would doing it good enough serve the purpose?

As you develop your plans and start to implement them, and you find yourself procrastinating or feeling blocked, remember to listen to your inner voice. Is it critical? Is it worried about how you will look or if you'll be embarrassed? If so, simply move from the first to the third person, remember what purpose the project serves, and get your ego out of the way. So much more can be accomplished.

Optimism and Determination: Valuable Resources

Imagination lays the tracks for the Reality Train... We do not need more power, magic or wealth, but rather to use the abundance we already possess in conscious, imaginative ways.

~ Caroline Casey

☙❧

Optimism and determination are valuable traits. Even the president of Gallup, the preeminent polling organization, recently stated:

> *Entrepreneurs have the rare gifts of optimism and determination, which are, and probably will remain, the new most valuable resources in the world. Optimism and determination are more valuable in the equation than creativity and innovation because they are rarer.*

As an entrepreneur, I know that it takes a great deal of optimism and determination to transition from being an employee fulfilling someone else's purpose to forging a self-directed new career focused on one's own purpose. Being an astrologer, a profession that is sometimes ridiculed or completely disregarded, did not make the entrepreneurial step any easier.

From where does optimism and determination come? In my experience, it comes from the inner drive to make a contribution to the world on your own terms. The calling that bubbles up from inside, which you cannot ignore, is a "Soul-inspired livelihood."

Though optimism and determination can elude me at times, even when self-doubt overrides, there is no way I could go back to a salaried job. I followed my heart's call six years ago and never looked back.

Do you feel optimistic and determined in what you do? If you feel irritated and your work does not express your inner values and motivations, consider formulating a plan to work toward answering your heart's call. It may call you into entrepreneurship or to another form of work, but don't waste your precious life feeling unfulfilled.

My worst days as an entrepreneur have all been better than my best days as an employee. That could be true for you, too. Whatever you do, may you be optimistic and determined most of the time!

It's Never Too Late to Follow Your Passion

I don't want to get to the end of my life and find that I lived just the length of it. I want to have lived the width of it as well.

~ Diane Ackerman

❧ ❧

When I was interviewed by MSN Money for a video website article titled, "Get Your Dream Job … at 55," I delighted in sharing how I left my corporate job to become an astrologer. It seems that many Baby Boomers, who are nearing retirement, have a desire to finally follow their passion after years of denying it.

For more than 25 years, I had valued and used astrology for personal guidance. Eventually, I became determined to know how astrologers were able to provide me with accurate information. At what were they looking? How did they do what they do?

My curiosity led me to study casually for many years while I was employed by someone else. After eight years of practicing astrology part time, I reached a point where I could no longer find meaning in my corporate job. Even then, it never occurred to me that I could make a career out of what I love: astrology.

Having grown up in a blue-collar family, I was taught that work was just that—work. If you wanted to have fun, you did it after you finished your job. I was preprogrammed to expect no satisfaction or enjoyment in my career.

My fear was that, if I took what I loved and made it an everyday task by making it my career, it would take the joy out of it. *Wrong!*

That did not happen. It is a miracle that I get paid for doing what I love to do: helping people appreciate their Soul's journey and bringing more joy and fulfillment into their lives.

My life has proven that it's never too late to follow your passion. When I counsel clients and friends about career concerns, I like to remind them that life has meaning and purpose and so do they. Have you discovered your unique purpose?

If you are not doing your passion, contributing your skills and abilities toward work that makes your heart sing, then you may be contributing to disharmony and distress in the world. If we all worked at what makes our heart sing, this would be one harmonious planet—a symphony of wonderful tones coming from happy, fulfilled people.

It is not too late to discover and do your passion!

Work as Service

What we do for ourselves dies with us. What we do for others and the world remains and is immortal.

~ Albert Pike, biographer of Mark Twain

❧ ❧

Certainly not everyone views their work as an act of service. Yet, when you see everything in life as interdependent, it becomes apparent that work—in its truest meaning—is *an act of serving others by expressing yourself through your skills and abilities.*

Growing up, I remember, my stay-at-home mom complained about doing the laundry and picking up after us. Dad would drag in the door and barely move from his chair all night. I observed that adults appeared to be burdened and complained about what they had to do.

By the time I was in my mid-30s, I had two jobs—an office worker by day and a housewife and mother by night—acting out the "work-is-work" approach they taught me.

In reality, work is not something separate from living. It is, in fact, a key component of your life. You spend many more hours working than in any other activity; if you don't feel fulfilled, you are wasting your precious life.

You may say, "A person has to earn a living." I suggest that, if you do not feel satisfaction and fulfillment in your work, you are really "earning a dying." Why shouldn't your work give you energy and increase your joy of living rather than seem like you are "earning a dying"?

"Work that gives you life" is not a contradiction in terms. When you are doing what you love—what your heart calls you to do—and using your unique skills and abilities, you feel fulfilled and enlivened, not drained and burdened.

I can say this because I have proved this in my own life. I find joy and fulfillment in my work as an astrologer and a writer. All areas of my life have been thriving as a result.

Do you wake up most mornings dreading your work day? If so, you are probably not doing your unique mission and purpose. If you are not doing what makes your heart sing, you dishonor yourself. The whole world is also suffering because it is missing your important contribution: *your* unique skills and abilities.

When you are doing work that makes your heart sing, and doing it to the best of your ability, you are doing work that is a service to all of us.

As humanity evolves, I envision that there will be a huge transformation in how and where work is done. The Soul-deadening, narrowly defined "cubicle" jobs inside corporations and other large organizations will become less and less desirable, while entrepreneurs, sole proprietors, and loosely organized business alliances will thrive.

Then we will be entering the era of "Soul-driven livelihood."

Valuing Time as a Contribution

Men resemble the gods in nothing so much as in doing good to their fellow creatures.

~ Cicero

꿍ꚿ

People of goodwill have a natural desire toward philanthropy. When we give to others, it helps remind us of all the bounty we have. In fact, if you are not feeling abundant, you are unlikely to think you have anything to give.

Yet, the time when you *aren't* feeling abundant is paradoxically the best time to give. Giving can shift your perspective about your own situation as you recognize the many with greater needs.

A dear friend recently expressed a desire for more financial prosperity so that she could give generously to her favorite cause. Ironically, this is the same friend who tirelessly gives many hours of service to that same cause. Hmm ... It seemed to me that she was already giving so much of her time.

Did she think that money counts but volunteer time does not? Of course, the U.S. tax system treats contributions this way, allowing a deduction for cash given but not for time served as a volunteer.

I believe that Spirit does not take such a money-centric approach. After all, money is just *one* measure of your time, talent, and effort contributed to producing a product or service. In my view, volunteer time and effort increases your "good karma" account just as much, if not more, than a cash contribution.

To get a truer view of your abundance and contributions to your favorite cause, consider what it would cost to hire such assistance.

For example, if you spend just eight hours a week making calls and holding meetings for your favorite cause, your contribution could be calculated as: 8 hours x \$12 (entry-level clerical) = \$96/week x 48 weeks in a year (remember to take vacation) = \$4,608.

Did you know that your contribution was that valuable? See how abundant you are!

A Good Deed Is Its Own Reward

Do good by stealth, and blush to find it fame.

~ Alexander Pope

᠀᠐᠀᠐

I have not always understood this adage by Alexander Pope. Frankly, it seemed to me that people should naturally notice the nice things I do. Why hadn't I been praised for doing such a noble action?

We are programmed to look for a reward for work given. Some call it a paycheck. Children are taught to say "thank you" when someone serves them. We call it "good manners." Yet, we do not fail to serve them if they do not say "thank you."

It is human nature to expect that, if you give, you will receive something in exchange, whether it is money, praise, or a pat on the back. However, should expectation of return determine what and when we will give?

Though a reward is nice, it is the internal good feelings of having done what felt right and meaningful that motivates continued giving. Perhaps internal validation fueled the giving of many now-famous people who received no recognition in their lifetime. It is funny how people have to die before they are praised for their accomplishments.

Recently, I discovered that Susan B. Anthony, the tireless campaigner for women's voting rights, never lived to enjoy the results of her work. The 19th Amendment was ratified 14 years after her death. She died without ever voting. What if she had decided that her actions were not worth doing unless she saw tangible results?

A recent movie, *Pay It Forward*, popularized the idea of doing random acts of kindness anonymously. Try it some time. Purposely perform a kind act so that it cannot be attributed to you and see how good it feels.

If you are living your life from the inside out (self-directed) rather than from the outside in (other-dependent), you will naturally understand that "a good deed *is* its own reward."

Social Change Without Blame

Fix the problem, not the blame.

~ Catherine Pulsifer

ॐ∽

From my view of the world, I see many actions—the way we treat one another locally, nationally, and globally—that could be more humane, more loving. Yet, for many years, I felt powerless to do anything. By observing the influence I have on others in my daily interactions, I now realize the influence I actually have.

The actions of one person can multiply like ripples in water as we interact with others. When we are aware of living in an interconnected, interdependent, sacred world, we know that what we do has an influence on others and the behavior of just one person does matter.

If I am you and you are me (inclusive thinking), I can no longer blame anyone else for the "mess" I see when I look out at the world. I am no longer a victim of others (e.g., corporations, governments, terrorists, or even my neighbor). Clearly, if I do not like the way "they" are behaving, it's up to me to create change by changing myself.

Blaming others for what we do not like is just another form of powerlessness. Blaming is what keeps the *status quo* in place.

Prior to the Iraq War, it was no secret that I did not favor the U.S. invasion of Iraq. While participating in an antiwar rally, I noticed that the signs people carried were often lettered with hate and personality-bashing slogans. The speakers spewed angry, complaining words about the war mongering and included a dozen other unrelated topics. I experienced the rally as one big festival of blaming—a gathering of victims.

Remembering that "what we resist persists," it dawned on me that everyone there who was blaming others and angry was adding to the energy perpetuating the march toward war.

Several weeks later, while participating in a prayer vigil on the Capitol grounds, the experience was remarkably different. I felt a deep peace as I recognized that my action added to the solution and not the problem. I demonstrated Gandhi's admonition to "be the change you wish to see in the world."

If you find yourself blaming someone, consider contributing to a solution by turning the spotlight on yourself. How are *you* being? Are you being what you wish to see in the world? Let what you are *being* change what you are *doing* and you *will* change the world!

"Happily Ever After" is Not the Goal

The search for happiness is one of the chief sources of unhappiness.

~ Zen saying

❧ ❦

People come to see me, as an astrologer, for many reasons. Sometimes a crisis or event has prompted them to seek a deeper perspective. Sometimes it is a feeling of being stuck with a need to find hope ahead. At other times, I serve to confirm what they already feel is true. Most people look for "good news" while "what they desire" is actually "what they mean."

What life presents can be so challenging to our carefully designed plans that it is easy to label any change as "bad." Yet, truly every experience in our lives is beneficial on our Soul's journey to wholeness.

Looking to find "happily ever after" is not good for your evolution. I know this as a result of my life experiences. Every challenge gave me a gift of greater awareness, which I would not have found without, at times, feeling great pain.

For example, a client of mine described her search for the ideal of total happiness: an end to all pain after Prince Charming swept her off her feet.

Sure, it would be absolutely delightful … for a while … but wouldn't it get boring if you always heard, "Yes, dear. Whatever you'd like, dear"?

The differences and the challenges in our relationships cause us to grow and evolve our understanding of who we are and what is important to us. A good relationship offers just enough challenges and differences of perspective that we are required to open our minds and hearts to growth and change.

By recognizing that the goal is not to live "happily ever after," we are able to keep an open mind and heart, which minimizes the pain that would come from holding on to a limited personal viewpoint.

If you find yourself seeking a "happily-ever-after" solution to your problems, think again. There is something to be learned and something to be gained from every challenge.

Chapter 6

Anticipating the Times Ahead

*With the breaking apart of old and crystallized forms of
civilization, the consciousness within those forms is released,
exposed to greater light, and freed to take on new forms that are
more appropriate to the currently unfolding stage of evolution.*

~ Nancy Siefer and Martin Viewig, *When the Soul Awakens*

Radical Transformation of Business and Government

The thing is, when Pluto is in Capricorn, we usually experience both sides. The good times come first, followed by the hard times, followed by redemption as we come back into touch with values and goals that are "good," and virtuous.

~ Ray Merriman, astrologer and financial market analyst

꙳

As I look ahead to anticipate the future, I use the lens that is most natural to me: astrology. You do not need to understand, believe in or agree with my conclusions. Let your Higher Self be your guide.

꙳

When Pluto moves from one sign to another, it is always big news. In 2008, the supposed "dwarf" planet moved from Sagittarius into Capricorn, where it will stay until 2024.

Despite Pluto's demotion to "dwarf" planet status, astrologers certainly have not changed their respect for the powerful societal transformation that occurs to matters ruled by the sign that Pluto inhabits at any particular time.

Pluto, with an odd elliptical path around the Sun, takes 246 years to complete one circuit. Pluto visits each sign during that time, but the length of time spent varies by sign. For example, Pluto spent 13 years in Sagittarius (1995-2008) and now has 16 years to transform all things related to Capricorn.

During the years when Pluto was in Sagittarius, we had to look at the dark side of fanaticism, when rigid belief systems (on both sides) led to religious and cultural conflicts. We saw the Catholic Church disgraced over pedophile priests and witnessed a split in the Episcopal Church over openly gay bishops. Relentless optimism and irrational exuberance, so typical of Sagittarius energy, helped fuel the housing bubble and runaway credit expansion.

Now with Pluto in Capricorn, we must adjust to a more grounded reality. We are being offered the opportunity to manifest the Sagittarian dreams if we are willing to do the Capricornian planning and hard work necessary to make it happen.

What can we expect from Pluto in Capricorn?

Capricorn rules large institutions such as government, corporations, and banks; buildings and infrastructure; and our drive toward success on the one hand and our pessimism and fear of scarcity on the other.

The last time Pluto was in Capricorn (1762-1778), it had not yet been discovered. The American Revolution, powered by anger over economic and taxation concerns (topics of concern today), sought to cut the cord with Mother England in favor of self-government.

Prior to that (1516-1533), Pluto in Capricorn powered Martin Luther's bold move for "religious independence" against a corrupt Catholic Church, which took money in exchange for a supposed easy time in heaven and led to the founding of the Protestant Church.

There is a theme here of "revolution" and "reformation." Reforming corrupt systems that no longer served the people was powered by the need to make evolutionary changes in government and economics. Fortunately, neither England nor the Catholic Church ceased to exist during the previous transits of Pluto... and neither will we.

Until 2024, Pluto's transformational processes may include:

+ Reform of the U.S. and other world governments (does anyone deny the need?)
+ Transformation of corporations into smaller, more innovative work units, with possible growth of entrepreneurship
+ Struggle and breakdown of the banking and monetary systems (fiat currency without backing) with possible return of precious metals as a foundation

Who knows what other aspects of business and government could be completely revised?

Rather than fear what is ahead, you can look forward to the changes. What would you like to see changed? Use your conscious intention by focusing on your wishes.

Here some possible areas where you can lend your creative intention by envisioning:

+ **New government:** How will it function? What needs to change? How can democracy function better? Could new mechanisms be developed to gather and act on citizens' input?
+ **New business:** How will business be done, both from the perspective of the consumer and the service or product provider? Could jobs become more meaningful, creative, and satisfying? Might employers

recognize the increasing importance of listening to input from their employees?

- **New economy:** In what way can we reorganize economics to provide more happiness and fulfillment for all? Could we reduce stress on the environment, increase community well-being, and ensure that we have needed resources by restoring greater community commerce in face-to-face relationships?

What about you personally? Here are some suggestions using vision and intention in your life:

- Move in new directions that bring you closer to living your purpose. Do strategic planning for implementing your goals.
- Release resentments or anything that might weigh you down from the past. Take responsibility for your own emotions.
- Let go of the illusion of your powerlessness. *You create your own reality.* Take responsibility for using your power.
- Detox your body, declutter your environment, downsize, and simplify. This leaves you with the freedom from worries that may prevent you from serving others by offering your gifts.
- Don't despair ... prepare! Create your vision of desired outcome and take the steps that lead to manifesting them every day.
- Consider who are your natural allies and reach out to them. Learn how to collaborate to succeed in win/win relationships.

We need not fear change. Every ending is a new beginning. This happens every day—when the Sun goes down and the Moon shines forth, only to bow to the Sun as it rises again the next day.

∂∽⬦

The reasonable man adapts himself to the world; the unreasonable one persists in trying to adapt the world to himself. Therefore, all progress depends on the unreasonable man.

~ George Bernard Shaw, playwright

Release and Let Flow

If we are growing, we're always out of our comfort zone.

~ John Maxwell

ॐॐॐ

Flooded with stories emphasizing fear and uncertainty, the daily news has become a barometer signaling whether we should feel hopeful today (a rarity) or whether we should sink back into despair.

At this point in human history, we find ourselves imbedded in turmoil and needing to recognize and face the huge changes ahead. Familiar sources of security and comfort are being altered by the need for evolutionary change. Though we may hope that things will calm down and return to "the way things were," that is not going to happen ... nor should it.

It is futile to try and cling like a capsized boater to a rock that caused the situation in the first place. What then can we do to save ourselves?

Though politicians, economists, or futurists will give you answers, my perspective is very different. As an astrologer, I have known for some time that this period (2008-2015) would be ripe for turbulent change, leading to major transformation in society. Contemplating how we might best manage our lives during this profound time of change, I have chosen to go within.

Remember: In every moment that you are feeling concern, the best way to find peace and restore joy is by listening to your own inner voice. You may consult others, but *your own inner voice (Higher Self or Soul) is the source of every answer and available in every moment.*

What I hear from my inner voice is, "Release, release ... release!"

Release every concept of the way life ought to be (i.e., the way you ought to be or the way others ought to be). Stop fighting with present reality!

Of course, you can hold an intention of what you would like, but then you must let it go in order to open to the flow of life, which is always bringing you the highest good in every moment, even though it may be disguised as suffering. Suffering? Oh, no, *not that!*

Suffering can be a "wake-up call" and an opportunity to make the changes that bring us closer to self-love, self-acceptance, and inner harmony, which translate into harmonious human relations and happiness in the outer world. Most suffering is simply a result of battling with current reality.

Just as the farmer has to plow the field and turn over the soil in order to prepare the ground for new crops, we are now moving toward a time of fertile change. We need to take heart and remember that the *breakdowns* we will be living through are leading to *breakthroughs* to a new phase of human existence on Earth, the likes of which we can only imagine.

Let life flow without grasping to keep things the same. Holding on creates suffering. When life doesn't change, it is called "death." To move through this profound time of change, it is imperative that you release, let go, and flow through every moment of the day.

Crisis = Opportunity to Find New Directions

... many people have felt the call to go deep within themselves and discover how their life can unfold in a deeper and more authentic way. As we are being realigned as a species, we are also finding new directions in our individual lives that will take us into a more defined relationship with the core of our being. The more anchored we become within ourselves, the stronger our foundation becomes and the better we are able to manage times of crisis.

~ Lynn Hayes, astrologer

ॐ ॐ

What an incredible time we are living through! Lynn Hayes' words above remind me that the Chinese symbol for *crisis* also has the dual meaning of *opportunity*.

Within the growing crises of environmental decay (e.g., global climate change and species extinction), economic decay (e.g., the housing bubble, excess debt, and unstable currencies) and lack of faith in leadership lies the *opportunity* for a better world.

As we move through times of crisis into a new world, we will find answers that lead us in *new directions*—not in old, well-trodden paths. The new directions will lead inwardly first ("What is my purpose?" "Why am I here?") and then outwardly ("Who do I care about?" "How can I be of service?")

Wall Street Sends a Wake-up Call

Enough is as little as possible and as much as necessary.

~ Unknown

❧ ❧

As for Wall Street's bank failures, buy-outs, and rescue plans, it's enough to make you want to stay in bed and pull the covers over your head, right? Think again.

This is only a surprise if you believe that life should always include more money, more things, more personal investments, more cars, more houses ... *whoa!* That is where the trouble originated. Speculation and greed have gotten the better of us and it is time to pay the piper.

I do not enjoy knowing that many people are suffering as housing values drop like a stone (my own daughter and her family got caught with a subprime mortgage that ballooned). This is just the beginning of challenges that will come in waves as we move through the next five to seven years.

If you think I am trying to alarm you, I am not.

Here's my message: Your best approach is to get your needs and your wants sorted out. You will always be able to find a way to fulfill what you *need*. By setting aside what you *want*—but don't necessarily need— and simplifying, your life will release undreamed-of space for a more harmonious, love-filled existence. Things such as family, friends, nature, and sunsets will find a higher presence within your value system.

Reach out to ask for help when you need it. Offer help whenever you can. There will be enough for everyone *as long as it is shared.*

The sky is not falling. It may be turning a new shade, however—one that will ultimately be more enjoyable to view.

Become a Pragmatic Mystic

People with high levels of personal mastery do not set out to integrate reason and intuition. Rather, they achieve it naturally as a by-product of their commitment to use all the resources at their disposal. They cannot afford to choose between reason and intuition, or head and heart any more than they would choose to walk on one leg or see with only one eye.

~ Peter Senge, Massachusetts Institute of Technology author/lecturer

∂∽⟋

The world is in desperate need of more pragmatic mystics. As we move through the next several years, the pragmatic mystics will survive and thrive.

Has the truth of our dilemma crashed the party of your dreams, or have your spiritual aspirations had trouble manifesting in outer form?

To be successful as we move into these times of change, it is necessary to balance pragmatic realism with visionary mysticism. Yet, they are two very different energies and, at first glance, would seem impossible to reconcile. That is why most people become strongly identified with one end of the seesaw more than the other.

Are you highly responsible? Do the words "duty," "tradition," and "patience" have more meaning than "creativity," "possibility," and "hope"? Then you may have been riding the *pragmatic* end of the seesaw.

If the "vision thing" has been your guide while you wait and hope for a break, then you are caught at the *mystical* end of the seesaw.

My life has been a search for how to merge the *ideal* with the *real* (i.e., the *spiritual* with *everyday matters*). I learned that life can be joyless and lacking in satisfaction without merging the two.

We are at a point in human evolution when neither the wisdom of mystics in a cave nor the security of your bank account alone can provide you with happiness.

Rather, we need to integrate our spiritual values into our work in the world. When we do meaningful work that makes our heart sing and meets the world's needs, we can also expect to thrive. To do this, we need to merge the *ideal* with the *real* and become a pragmatic mystic!

Ground and Implement Your Vision

Turning it over in your mind won't plough the field.

~ Irish saying

⤫

In the midst of stress between old ways and new possibilities, how can we consciously move forward with ease and in harmony with the energy of the times?

As traditions conflict with innovations for a brighter future, we need a vision that is grounded. Insights for the future also need step-by-step instructions for how to get there. How do you develop instructions to get to a place you have never been before?

If the clarion call is to take your innovative vision and make it tangible and practical, what would it look like?

Here are some of the themes that are becoming apparent to me:

- **Self-responsibility:** It is no longer appropriate to look for someone to take care of us, like a father figure to tell us what is "right." *Use your own wisdom and inner guidance.* Everyone has the ability to go within for answers. Your guidance knows your purpose and your path better than anyone else outside you.
- **Action:** Take time to listen to your dreams, hopes, and even fears, but don't leave it there. *Actualize* possibilities.
- **Focus:** Don't fall prey to the distraction of multiple options. Endless variety and more information than a lifetime could absorb are readily available. Focus on what is truly important and do not get distracted.
- **Commitment:** It is easy to chase rainbows, moving from one to another and never having to deal with the consequences of our behavior. Commitment to an ideal and the willingness to remain on the ground for the long haul are needed.
- **Detachment:** If you let self-criticism immobilize you, nothing will ever get better and the future will be more of the same. *Get out of your own way.*
- **Interdependence:** All wisdom does not reside in one person. Reach out to others and create change that affects the good of the Whole

by gathering with like-minded people. Don't waste your vision. Share it with others.

As we move through times of profound change, conscious people who are grounded and working to implement their vision in the flow of evolutionary change will co-create a really new human existence on Earth.

Know Your Rudder

One needs something to believe in, something for which one can have whole-hearted enthusiasm. One needs to feel that one's life has meaning, that one is needed in this world.

~ Hannah Senesh

છે જી

When we are tired of the bad news, and when change is forcing us out of ruts, vice-like pressure of resistance can create earthquakes—literally and figuratively speaking.

What can you do to meet and manage the changes ahead? One of the most important things you will need to thrive through this profound period in human history is a true sense of your own unique purpose.

In the changing times ahead, you must know and keep your hand on your "rudder."

Your life purpose or mission is like a rudder guiding the direction of your life. Knowing why you are here will guide and direct your life choices. Without it, your life is fated to be blown about by the winds of change, at the mercy of outer turbulence.

Do you know why you were born? What is your unique purpose and mission? Think of it as your gift to humanity—that special perspective, skill, or ability that makes your heart sing when you express it.

When the uncertainties of the future loom large, it is by knowing and focusing on your personal mission that you will find the day-to-day grounding necessary to keep moving forward with a sense of joy and fulfillment. Remembering why you are here can give your life meaning at any time but, during times of social upheaval, it is essential.

If you don't know or are unsure about it, how do you find your rudder? Here are some suggestions:

+ Go inside and ask your inner guidance to tell you.
+ Consider your unique gifts, probably the ones you take for granted since they come easily to you.
+ Arrange an astrological consultation to understand your Soul's purpose.
+ Consult with a life coach or spiritual mentor.

There may be other tools and techniques that are useful. Keep in mind that your life purpose may not be a skill to develop as much as it is a trait that you express naturally.

Several years ago, my inner voice told me my mission was "to teach self-love by honoring the uniqueness in each individual." I had not yet begun doing astrological consultations, so I wondered how I could do that. What would it look like? I now realize that is exactly what I am doing in my private sessions and in my writing.

In actuality, I have always had the desire to encourage and support others. It had been so natural that I failed to recognize it as a talent and my purpose.

In the months and years ahead, knowing what your "rudder" or purpose is will assist you in making decisions and taking actions that ultimately help you thrive. In fact, living "on purpose" is one of the major changes being urged at this time. It is the way you will contribute to making this a better world for all of us.

Jalaluddin Rumi, a 13th century philosopher and poet, offers us this reminder:

The One Thing You Must Do

There is one thing in this world which you must never forget to do. If you forget everything else and not this, there's nothing to worry about, but if you remember everything else and forget this, then you will have done nothing in your life.

It's as if a king has sent you to some country to do a task, and you perform a hundred other services, but not the one he sent you to do. So human beings come to this world to do particular work. That work is the purpose, and each is specific to the person.

If you don't do it, it's as though a priceless Indian sword were used to slice rotten meat. It's a golden bowl being used to cook turnips, when one filing from the bowl could buy a hundred suitable pots. It's like a knife of the finest tempering nailed into a wall to hang things on.

You say, "Look, I'm using the dagger. It's not lying idle." Do you hear how ludicrous that sounds? For a penny an iron nail could be bought to serve for that.

You say, "I spend my energies on lofty enterprises, I study jurisprudence and philosophy and logic and astronomy and medicine and all the rest." Consider why you do those things. They are all branches of yourself.

Remember the deep root of your being, the presence of your Lord.

Give your life to the one who already owns your breath and your moments.

If you don't, you will be exactly like the man who takes a precious dagger and hammers it into his kitchen wall for a peg to hold his dipper gourd.

You'll be wasting valuable keenness and foolishly ignoring the dignity of your purpose.

Weather the Storm with Cooperation and Listening

You are used to listening to the buzz of the world but now is the time to develop the inner ear that listens to the inner world. It is time to have a foot in each world, and it can be done.

~ Bartholomew

ھو

You would have to be a hermit not to realize that, since late 2007, the entire world has entered a phase of upheaval and change. The prevailing mood is saturated with fear as huge cracks appear in the foundation of our economic life.

The time of the "lone wolf" is over and the start of a new ethic—based on collaboration and a sense of community—is beginning. After all, an economic system that runs on competition and greed really needs to transform, if we want to survive and thrive, on this increasingly interconnected planet.

Beware of those who wish everything would return to normal. Whatever "normal" was, we are not likely to return to anything like we remember from the past—*nor should we.*

In the next several years, we will be transforming our social, political, and economic landscape ... an exciting opportunity to create a better society.

For everyone, it provides an opportunity to let go of fear and panic while allowing new values—cooperation, sharing, and reverence for life—to emerge. Now is the time to find and heal the sources of fear within you and release the love buried beneath.

This is a call for evolutionary growth. Those who step up to the task and make really new and courageous choices will, I believe, weather the challenge of economic winter and ultimately enjoy the growth opportunities of spring.

Consider personally preparing by redefining "needs" versus "desires." Cut loose erroneous assumptions of what you deserve, addictions to past excesses, flawed self-concepts, illusion, and delusions, and do things in a more pragmatic and practical manner.

Listen to your own inner wisdom as you evaluate what truly has meaning for you (your needs) versus what may be frivolous or transient (your desires).

Then notice the positive changes that result from refocusing your compass toward a more practical and cooperative future.

Happiness from Enough

Happiness consists not in having, but of being, not of possessing, but of enjoying. It is the warm glow of a heart at peace with itself.

~ Norman Vincent Peale

❧ ❦

As I write, the U.S. unemployment rate is hovering around 10 percent; perhaps half again as many people are underemployed. It is difficult for many to find a reason to be happy. Perhaps, at times like these, it will help to revisit the meaning of happiness and where it is found. As the Peale quote above describes, happiness "consists not in having, but of being, not of possessing, but of enjoying."

Could it be that just "being" and "enjoying" are the source of happiness?

It appears that happiness is not found outside us. It is not found in a paycheck, a bank balance, or a house with a certain number of square feet. No, indeed. It is not found in anything external to us.

Fortunately, I have come to know the truth: *Happiness is an inside job.* I remember the moment when I realized that happiness is a *choice.* I realized that I could see my circumstances as a glass half empty or choose to see the glass as half full. Since that day when I chose the half-full glass, it has gotten fuller and fuller. Some days, my glass runs over with joy!

My happiness has grown in direct proportion to my awareness of having "enough" of what I need in every moment.

In this moment, consider this: Do you have enough of what you need? Not what you would like or desire, but what you need.

In the next few years, as we move through this transformational time when economics, business, and government are undergoing major restructuring, it will be increasingly important to our continued survival and happiness to recognize what is *enough.*

Perhaps the excesses of the past—when it seemed like happiness came from the exotic vacations, hot cars, designer clothes, or newest technologies—need to fade into disillusionment. Out of our losses, a whole new value system will arise from within, based on an understanding of happiness as coming from *enough.*

What if our core values are being completely transformed for the better? It only looks like an economic crisis at the moment (and it certainly is for those without enough food or shelter) but, in reality, it is a *spiritual plot* to awaken humanity to the true source of happiness—"being" and "enjoying"—that moves from within outward into our daily life as a reunion of Spirit in the matters of our daily life.

The End is Coming or Could It Be a Beginning in 2012?

Have you found the beginning, then, that you are looking for the end? You see, the end will be where the beginning is.

~ Jesus in *The Gospel of Thomas*

෯෪

It is said that the Mayan calendar's current cycle will be ending on the Winter Solstice, December 21, 2012. The calculations for the end of their 5,125-year world age have awakened the fear of many who actually believe the world might be physically coming to an end.

Hollywood, of course, has seized the opportunity to cash in with a blockbuster movie, which plays to the fear that "the end is coming." Even the Discovery Channel presents the possibilities in crisis terms.

Yet, as an astrologer, this much I know: Every cycle has a beginning and an end; then, there is a *new* beginning that will also end.

The really interesting fact is that all cycles also lie within other cycles like the "fractals" that Greg Braden writes about in his book, *Fractal Time*. He, too, agrees that the end of the Mayan calendar is significant but not to be feared.

What if it ushers in a profoundly new stage in human evolution?

Just as we know from the monthly cycle of the Moon, there is a dark sky just before and after the New Moon. The great promise of what is possible to manifest by the Full Moon cannot be seen but only imagined. That is why for eons people have wished upon the New Moon for those things they want to manifest by the Full Moon.

So, too, as we live through the next several years, it is impossible to know exactly what will happen, and yet it is a perfect time to create a vision of what is desirable and begin to make it happen.

Meanwhile, just as it is a bit scary when you enter a dark room, we can expect to have moments of insecurity and confusion. The unknown is always disconcerting and often frightening.

To process the feelings that may come up as a result of the breakdowns and breakthroughs ahead, answer the following questions:

+ Where have I been holding rigid beliefs that have outlived their usefulness?
+ Where am I too idealistic?

- Which of my goals need to be revised and redefined to better match the reality in which I find myself?
- What fears are keeping me from trusting myself and my Source?
- How can I be more compassionate with myself and my limitations?
- How might I deepen my spiritual connection with Spirit and notice its expression in my life?

The end is coming and so is the beginning. Make the most of what is ahead by staying grounded in the moment and being willing to explore what lies ahead.

Afterword

Life is always offering expanded awareness, if you are open. If you think there is somewhere that you must arrive, you will be disappointed because life is always unfinished business. Enjoy the journey!

Above all, remember that you are not alone. You are a part of an awakening "community of Souls" who are bringing Spirit into everyday life.

Even if you have not yet found that community, it is still possible that, one day through opening up to Spirit's presence, you will recognize kindred Souls and together forge a new way of living on Earth.

Thich Naht Hanh gives us this vision:

> It is possible that the next Buddha will not take the form of an individual. The next Buddha may take the form of a community—a community practicing understanding and loving kindness, a community practicing mindful living. This may be the most important thing we can do for the survival of the Earth.

Bibliography

Abdullah, Sharif. *Creating a World That Works for All*. Barrett-Koehler, 1999.

Adams, Dianne Eppler. *Flip Negatives to Positives: Tips for Thriving in Change and Uncertainty*. Spirit in Matters. 2009. <www.SpiritinMatters.com/products.html>

Bauman, Bill. *Soul Vision: A modern mystic looks at life through the eyes of the soul*. The Center for Soulful Living, 2009.

Braden, Gregg. *Fractal Time: The Secret of 2012 and a New World Age*. Hay House, 2009.

Byrne, Rhonda. *The Secret*. Atria Books/Beyond Words, 2006.

A Course in Miracles. Foundation for Inner Peace, 1975.

Dyer, Dr. Wayne W. *The Power of Intention*. Hay House, 2005.

Jampolsky, Gerald G. *Love is Letting Go of Fear*. Celestial Arts, 2004.

Kinslow, Frank. *Beyond Happiness: How You Can Fulfill Your Deepest Desire*. Lucid Sea, 2008.

McLaughlin, Corinne and Gordon Davidson. *Spiritual Politics: Changing the World from the Inside Out*. Ballantine Books, 1994.

Moore, Thomas. *Care of the Soul: A Guide for Cultivating Depth and Sacredness in Everyday Life*. HarperPerennial, 1994.

Myss, Carolyn. *Sacred Contracts: Awakening Your Divine Potential*. Harmony Books, 2001.

Ohotto, Robert. *Transforming Fate into Destiny: A New Dialogue With Your Soul*. Hay House, 2008.

Franklin, Benjamin. *Poor Richard's Almanac*. Skyhorse Publishing, 2007.

Ruiz, Don Miguel. *The Four Agreements: A Practical Guide to Personal Freedom, A Toltec Wisdom Book*. Amber-Allen, 2001.

Shimhoff, Marcy. *Happy for No Reason: 7 Steps to Being Happy from the Inside Out*. Free Press, 2009.

Siefer, Nancy and Martin Vieweg. *When the Soul Awakens: The Path to Spiritual Evolution and a New World Era*. Gathering Wave Press, 2009.

Tolle, Eckhart. *A New Earth: Awakening to Your Life's Purpose*. Penguin, 2005.

Appendix

Using Astrology as a Conscious Tool

An unfailing experience of mundane events
in harmony with the changes occurring in the heavens,
has instructed and compelled my unwilling belief.

~ Johannes Kepler

Note: The use of astrology is not for everyone. Just as there are multitudes of ways to realize the Divine, there are also many other tools to assist us as we travel the spiritual path. What follows are answers to questions that explain why an intelligent person in the 21st century might choose to use astrology as a conscious tool.

What is Astrology?

That which is Below corresponds to that which is Above, and that which is Above corresponds to that which is Below, to accomplish the miracles of the One Thing.

~ Hermes Trismegistus, *Law of Correspondence*

ॐॐ

Astrology is an ancient symbolic language that recognizes the universe as an indivisible whole and a method of exploring who we are, our relationships, and our role within the world. The word is derived from the Greek words *astron,* meaning "star," and *logos,* meaning "word." Literally, it means the "language of the stars."

Just as Egyptian hieroglyphics refer to concepts far more complex than a single word could convey, planetary symbols and movements are rich with layered meanings.

Astrology works by looking at the relationships of the heavenly bodies at the exact time and place of birth, and deriving symbolic meaning from the archetypal energies represented by the position of the planets at that moment.

Astrology can provide insight into any situation—from the personal to the political, and from the most intimate to the most mundane. In addition, understanding the archetypal energies in the future can help you better exercise your free will by making decisions in harmony with the energies of the time.

If you read your magazine or newspaper horoscope and think that is all there is to astrology, you are deceived. What you find can be shallow and too general for anything more than entertainment.

Real astrology is not entertainment. When done well, astrology is a serious tool that can provide important insights for your life's journey. It describes the physical, emotional, intellectual, and spiritual challenges and opportunities you will encounter as you go through your life.

Professional astrologers have studied many years; some, like me, may have obtained certification from one of several professional astrological organizations. They may be specialized in a particular technique or type of astrology such as Western, Vedic, Hellenistic, or Medieval, or have a particular focus such as relationship, career, financial, or health.

The Greeks believed the stars do not *define* us, they *incline* us. I agree, and view the planetary influences as "energies" to which we may respond in a variety of ways. If doing so unconsciously, we may struggle; if consciously, we may still struggle, but grow wiser.

What is the History of Astrology?

Astrology represents the summation of all the psychological knowledge of antiquity.

~ Carl G. Jung

❧

Astrological knowledge has developed over more than 5,000 years of observation. The constellations were likely established around 3,000 BCE. The oldest horoscope chart dates to 410 BCE; however, 2,000 years before that (in Mesopotamia), sky omens were used by kings to consider the probable success or failure of military actions.

The Greeks, such as Hippocrates, used astrology for medical diagnosis. It was also used for determining the best time to plant. Even today, astrology is one of the sources of information for the *Farmer's Almanac*.

Fearing that star knowledge could not be controlled, Roman emperor Constantine outlawed astrology in 312 CE; in 400 CE, St. Augustine condemned it.

As Europe entered the Dark Ages, astrological knowledge was transferred to the Islamic world where fortunately it was preserved. As a result of the flowering of the Renaissance, beginning in the 14th century, ancient astrological knowledge was revived from Islamic sources and became strong again.

Many prominent astronomers were also astrologers. In 1404 CE, Copernicus was actually required to do a yearly astrological forecast to maintain his teaching position at the University of Bologna.

Even though Galileo's telescope confirmed Copernicus' theory that the Earth revolves around the Sun—a fact later used to discredit astrology—Galileo himself was capable as an astrologer.

Sadly, astrology fell out of favor after Galileo's proof. A once-prominent subject was no longer studied in universities, which allowed untrained charlatans to begin mixing astrology with questionable forms of the occult, and its use declined.

A little known fact is that Benjamin Franklin, one of the American founding fathers, was also an astrologer. For 25 years, Franklin wrote and published *Poor Richard's Almanac*. In the first edition, printed in 1733, his astrological knowledge was shown in the beginning article titled "The Names and Characters of the Seven Planets." (This was before the discovery of Uranus, Neptune, and Pluto.)

Revived around the turn of 20th century, one of the most famous advocates of astrology was Carl Jung. He used astrology personally and probably used it to better understand the psychological issues of his patients. Jung's daughter became a prominent Swiss astrologer.

Since the 1960s, astrology has grown more reputable. Many new techniques and new knowledge have been added as a result of computers' ability to make complex research easier.

How Does Astrology Work?

Astrology is astronomy brought to earth and applied to the affairs of men.

~ Ralph Waldo Emerson

Knowledge of the workings of astrology has been accumulated over eons through observing the heavens. Although the exact mechanism that causes it to work is not fully understood, astrology has become known by its results.

Though astrology is often seen as implausible because the cause behind it cannot be explained, other unseen forces known only by their results (e.g., electricity and magnetism) have long been accepted by science.

If one accepts the commonly-held belief that the Moon's cycle has an effect on the tides on Earth, it is not a huge leap to suggest that other planetary influences—undiscovered or unmeasured— are operating. Regardless, astrology's results speak loudly to those who appreciate symbols and archetypes.

Planets represent different energies or behaviors. The signs describe the way the planets express their meaning, like the lens through which the planets see and act. The 12 houses in the horoscope represent locations or fields of experience. In this way, astrology gives a framework of meaning, allowing us to consciously engage with life and its happenings.

What is a birth chart?

The birth chart or "horoscope" is a map of the heavens at the precise moment and exact place of birth and includes the Sun, Moon, and planets. Asteroids and fixed stars may also be used, depending on the astrologer's preference.

The significance of the birth chart is based on the idea that whatever is born at a particular moment in time possesses the qualities of that moment. Thus, the birth chart is a map or blueprint in symbolic form of the moment a person, a relationship, a business, or even a city or country was born.

Do you have to believe in astrology to make use of it?

No, you do not have to believe in astrology to find it useful. No one would say you have to believe in art to enjoy it. By the same token, you don't have to believe in gravity, but it keeps you on the ground anyway.

What is an astrological consultation?

An astrology consultation is an interactive process or conversation between an astrologer and a client. The astrologer helps the client take advantage of opportunities and timing, cope with distress, or understand and solve personal problems.

The process utilizes the astrologer's astrological knowledge, life experience, and communication skills, which is why finding the right person is important. It should be someone whose life experiences have given them sufficient wisdom so they are able to offer you new awareness for your own life.

Be sure to share your issue or concern openly as soon as you have established trust in the astrologer. An astrologer is not necessarily psychic (though some may be), so holding back details will not serve your highest good.

The archetypal symbols in the chart are revealed through dialogue. Awareness of the level of consciousness operating within the symbols is missing from the chart. By the chart alone, an astrologer cannot tell whether you are paying attention as you live or are just sleepwalking through life.

What can be seen by the astrologer are themes or issues occurring currently or in the future that you may need to address. Like a spiritual or visionary coach, the astrologer can help the client envision possible choices that can be made to co-create the future in harmony with the energies evident in the chart.

No astrologer can accurately predict exactly what will happen; if they do, it could become a self-fulfilling prophecy. Rather, it is best viewed like an extended weather report—your personal cosmic weather ahead.

While clients may talk about everyday issues, I am aware what I am talking about is how Spirit is operating in their lives. For me, all of life is sacred, and Spirit is in the midst of every issue or concern, no matter how mundane it seems.

❧⚜

How can you benefit from consulting an astrologer?

Using a nonjudgmental approach, the astrologer can help frame your issues in the context of a higher power and open up a deeper meaning of events, thus helping you discover your place in the universe.

When we know the duration of various cycles, we can more easily endure the difficult times, understanding the period of beginnings and endings as we go through life's cycles of learning.

An astrological consultation can help you recognize your strengths, provide insight into your life issues, confirm self-knowledge, suggest your life purpose, reveal periods of crisis and opportunity, and provide guidance as to timing for choosing a course of action.

You will discover that you are a perfect expression of the energies of your birth moment. Your gifts and challenges are unique. As a result, you will better appreciate how special you are, thus aiding self-esteem and self-love.

❧⚜

Why consult with an astrologer?

Here are some reasons to consult with an astrologer:

+ **Self-knowledge:** By confirming your awareness of who you are, an astrologer may help quiet self-criticism by highlighting the positive side of traits formerly viewed as negative. The astrologer's nonjudgmental comments honor your uniqueness. You are as unique and marvelous as a snowflake.
+ **Life purpose:** If you accept that life has meaning, then knowing your purpose can make navigating the challenges that much easier. Recognizing your part in the Divine Plan helps eliminate the fears and doubts that undermine trust in yourself, your instincts, and your interests.
+ **Career/finances:** Want to change jobs? Learn when it might be most favorable to send out resumes or to schedule interviews. Finances

can ebb and flow from time to time; by knowing ahead of time, you can prevent excesses when conservation is wiser.

+ **Optimum timing:** Are you planning a wedding, launching a business, signing a contract, or scheduling surgery? An astrologer can help you choose an optimum day and time for maximizing potential success.

+ **Relationship challenges/opportunities:** Compatibility concerns and the desire to better understand your lover, spouse, business partner, children, or coworkers motivate many to see an astrologer. Naturally, accepting other people's unique traits rather than expecting change is what brings harmony. If you are seeking a relationship, you can discover when the potential for meeting someone is strongest.

+ **Personal planning:** At New Year, or at the time of your birthday, it is common to consult an astrologer. Through a review of your personal cycles for the year ahead, you can be prepared for a more thoughtful exercise of your free will, making decisions in harmony with the energies seeking to be expressed at the time.

+ **Health:** Concerns about health and healing, surgery, and even fertility optimization can be addressed with astrology. Often, the chart will show that physical symptoms are really emotional issues that have been avoided long enough to have weakened your body. Awareness of underlying issues along with good medical care can lead to a cure.

Information provided by an astrologer can help you make difficult decisions, but you cannot expect your astrologer to make your decisions for you. That is your job.

Remember: You always have the right and responsibility to make your own choices and to ignore any of the astrologer's advice that does not ring true for you. It is your responsibility to filter what is being said through your own "inner truth detector."

☙❧

DO go to an astrologer if

+ You are seeking greater harmony and purpose in your life. The information received can aid you in making decisions and taking actions in sync with your unique personal cycles.

- You want a better understanding of who you are and what your purpose is so you can live your life to the fullest.
- You wish for greater relationship compatibility. The road to healthy relationships is through self-understanding.
- You desire to choose the optimum time for something important, like getting married, starting a business, scheduling surgery, or selling a house.

DO NOT go to an astrologer if

- You need someone to solve your problems for you. An astrologer may provide information that can be quite insightful, but you are responsible for and capable of solving your problems and choosing your future.
- You have deeply held fears and insecurities. You would be better served to consult a psychotherapist. Astrologers are not psychotherapists, though some psychotherapists are also astrologers.

God Created Astrology

The heavens are telling the glory of God; and the firmament proclaims his handiwork. Day to day pours forth speech, and night to night declares knowledge.

~ Psalms 19:1-2

∾∾

Astrology, it seems, is only now coming out of its own "dark ages." While most other intellectual and scientific fields rode a wave of advancement during the time of 18th century Enlightenment, astrology was reduced to a place of ridicule as a form of chicanery.

Science and religion, if they could not agree on anything else, at least agreed that astrology had no merit. It is interesting that such unity should exist between them, while in every other way science and religion were adversaries.

The fact that science and religion are now beginning to find some areas of agreement, and the fact that astrology is also finding renewed interest, is no coincidence. It is due, I believe, to the important role astrology has to play in the coming times for our understanding of life on Earth.

Astrology—in its holistic approach to the physical, emotional, mental, and spiritual cycles of life—is a bridge between the science of the physical world and the religion of the spiritual world.

In many parts of the world (e.g., Iraq, Iran, India, Tibet, and China), some form of astrology has long been accepted, especially where Hinduism and Buddhism are found. That is not true of regions where the religions of the Western world—Christianity and Judaism—are found. Yet, the religious basis of astrology can be found in the sacred literature of these religions: the Holy Bible.

In the first chapter of the Bible, Genesis 1:14, the fourth day of Creation is described: "And God said, 'Let there be lights in the firmament of the heavens to separate the day from the night, and let them be for **signs** [emphasis added] and for seasons and for days and years.'"

Before man was created, God set the heavenly bodies in the sky for "signs" or for what I see as guidance. The planets do not cause us to do things or control us but instead reveal the wisdom of Divine Intelligence that created both man and the heavenly bodies, as "signs."

Psalms 19:1-2 offer a celebration of the magnificence of the heavens and the wonder of their message and meaning: "The heavens are telling the glory of God; and the firmament proclaims his handiwork. Day to day pours forth speech, and night to night declares knowledge."

When you get a reading, astrologers are interpreting the "speech" and "knowledge" of the heavens.

Matthew, recording the significance of Jesus' birth, wrote of the visiting astrologers, also known as wise men (from present-day Iraq), who came to worship Jesus when he was born. They had been studying the heavens and came to Jerusalem saying, "Where is he who has been born King of the Jews? For we have seen his star in the East and have come to worship him." (Matthew 2:1-2)

Astrology played an important role in announcing Jesus' birth and proving his divinity. In fact, Jesus himself, when describing the time when he would return to Earth, indicated that "... there will be signs in Sun and Moon and stars." (Luke 21:25)

Some Christians condemn astrology as false prophesy, yet Paul urged in I Thessalonians 5:20-22: "... do not despise prophesying, but test everything, hold fast what is good, abstain from every form of evil."

In truth, astrology is no more a false prophecy than a weather report. Like the weatherman, an astrologer suggests what the "physical, emotional, intellectual, or spiritual weather" may be like in the coming months.

The ability to read "the signs in Sun and Moon and stars" provides insight into the timing of cycles. It is written that "... for everything there is a season, and a time for every purpose under heaven." (Ecclesiastes 3:1)

Understanding cycles increases your wisdom to exercise free will, to prepare for challenging times, and to seek balance during times of success and opportunity.

Indeed, God created astrology for our benefit to enhance our free will and to assist our ability to read the "signs" that He writes in the heavens for our evolving understanding of our lives and purpose on Earth.

Astrology and Fortune-Telling

Astrology is not an augury of fate; it's a practical, problem-solving tool.

~ Donna Cunningham, Skywriter blog

ॐॐ

The general population tends to lump astrologers with "fortune-tellers"—those who claim to know what will actually happen in the future. It is true that charlatans using all types of techniques have conned the weak and vulnerable into spending money and taking unwise actions based on their advice.

However, there is nothing unprincipled about considering the future by consulting knowledgeable experts, such as futurists, financial advisors, or even fashion consultants, for a prediction of *possibilities*.

When you tune into the weather forecast, aren't you expecting the meteorologist to predict the future? They give you their best guess of the weather ahead based on highly developed knowledge of weather patterns on Earth and the probabilities of a certain weather condition occurring. Astrology is quite similar.

Astrologers study the accumulated knowledge of over 5,000 years, gained from observation of planetary movements and the synchronicity of their actions with events in human affairs.

Looking at astrology and equating it with fortune-telling is problematic for astrologers.

Some conscious people may avoid consulting an astrologer because they don't want the future to be taken out of their hands or because they are afraid of bad news—as if your fate were in the hands of the astrologer. It is not.

Your future is always in your own hands, created one decision at a time. What the astrologer sees is simply whatever energies may be active in your life during a period of time.

As with the weather forecaster from whom you benefit by knowing if it will be rainy tomorrow and can then decide whether to take your umbrella, so, too, can you benefit by knowing, for example, that a period of financial restriction is coming. You might then forego unnecessary purchases and hold on to your resources, knowing that this will pass and approximately when it will pass.

Knowing the energies of the time allows you to better exercise your free will. You are able to make decisions in harmony with the energy of the moment.

Another way that equating astrology to fortune-telling is problematic is when people come to an astrologer hoping to know if they will win the lottery or how they should find their Soul mate. The truth is that you could pass through a highly favorable time for finding a relationship and, if you do not leave the house or put yourself in social situations, the possibility will pass without manifesting a partner.

The *outcomes* of the energies ahead are still determined by you, *not* the astrologer.

Do not go to an astrologer thinking that he or she can manage your life for you. You will be disappointed. You are always in charge of your life. No one can or should control your destiny!

There's another way that the question of fortune-telling is problematic for astrologers. In some cities, counties, and states across the nation, astrologers are prevented from practicing their profession by repressive laws—a profession once so prominent that Copernicus was *required* to do annual forecasts to keep his academic position!

Unfortunately, these repressive laws lump legitimate astrologers, who have years of study and extensive astronomical as well as astrological knowledge, along with questionable card, palm, or psychic readers.

I make no judgment of card, palm, or psychic readers. There are unscrupulous practitioners in any profession. The problem is that the perceived act of forecasting the future (e.g., what the meteorologist does on daily television) is prevented by some of these laws, rather than weeding out those practitioners who are disreputable.

When you think about astrology, do not think about fortune-telling. Think about *guidance for planning* the year ahead. Think about how this information could be *helpful in making choices* to navigate the constantly changing circumstances and relationships in your life.

When delivering news of a challenging time, a good astrologer will offer suggestions for navigating the rough waters ahead. You might call on a good astrologer to assist you just as you might choose a good tax accountant. Remember that, ultimately, your life is created by you ... one choice at a time.

Fate Versus Free Will

Free will is the willingness to do that which one must do.

~ Carl G. Jung

Destiny is something for which we must strive; fate is what happens to us if we don't. Both are visible in the birth chart.

~ Steven Forest, astrologer

☙ ❧

The question of fate versus free will has been explored for eons. It has been mental fodder for philosophers and other deep thinkers along with questions like "Who am I?" and "Why am I here?"

Whatever answers have been offered, what is accepted as true depends on the point of view of the individual reading it. I offer my own perspective with respect for the answer you have found and the decisions you have reached as a result of your life experiences.

Astrology is often viewed as fatalistic. Some say that, in order for it to work at all or make sense, astrology must therefore describe how fate is working in a person's life.

If you feel like a victim of fate, going to an astrologer could help confirm your dread or possibly illuminate your hopes.

For those who today are increasingly self-aware and believe that they create their own reality, going to an astrologer might seem like abdicating their responsibility for creating their own reality.

It is interesting to note that astrologers do not agree on this topic either. I, for one, do not believe that we are either "victims" of our fate nor completely free to create our lives.

For example, who by willing it can change the color of their eyes or the size of their feet? There are clearly some things about us that were fated before we were born. On the other hand, the career path you chose, although influenced by others (parents or peers), was an act of free will. You made the choice of what course to study, what school to attend, and what job offer to accept.

As I see it, there is no black-and-white answer to this question. At times, our lives feel fated—out of our own hands and perhaps guided by a greater force or wisdom; at other times, we create the circumstances of our lives through an act of will.

The balancing act of fate and free will, in my view, is determined by our level of consciousness and self-awareness. For example, I believe I was fated to become an astrologer, but the timing and circumstances that led to this were determined by my conscious choice to step into that role—a choice that took a long time coming.

For many years, I worked a variety of different jobs in a corporate setting. While my fascination with astrology grew and grew, my study deepened, and I finally began doing consultations on a part-time basis. There were many times when I might have begun a full-time practice, but I was not yet ready to step into the identity of being an "astrologer." Finally, the discomfort of not acting on my heart's calling became too great. The result? I left the corporate world and launched my business and new identity as an astrologer.

Was I fated to be an astrologer? I think so. However, I know it was my choice and my own free will that moved me to step forward into a full-time practice. I followed what had been my heart's calling all along.

Can you think of a time when you resisted an opportunity for change but later made a choice that had been there all along? I see this as the intersection of fate and free will, where consciousness made the difference.

I know every one of us has a purpose to fulfill. That purpose is a part of our very essence, yet it may have many possible ways or scenarios through which to be expressed. Life offers many options to do this. The path to our greatest joy comes from following the calling of our purpose. Astrology can provide a clearer understanding of your purpose.

Is your purpose fated? Perhaps, yet how you find your purpose, what you do with that awareness, and when and how you express your purpose are all a result of the exercise of your free will and the power of choice.

Your power of choice and free will is more intelligently expressed when you understand the underlying blueprint of your life. That blueprint is your astrological chart.

About the Author

Dianne Eppler Adams, CAP, is a certified astrological consultant in Alexandria, Virginia. Using a Western psychological-spiritual approach, she specializes in providing life-enhancing insights for people and businesses wishing to optimize their success and fulfillment by seeing the opportunity in change and uncertainty, paying particular attention to the uniqueness of each Soul's Journey.

Dianne is also the author of the e-book, *Flip Negatives to Positives: Tips for Thriving in Change and Uncertainty*, and writes a popular New Moon e-newsletter, *Spirit in Matters*.

Dianne has been certified by the International Society for Astrological Research and holds membership in the National Committee for Geocosmic Research, the Organization for Professional Astrology, and the Association for Astrological Networking.

Dianne is a member of and a speaker for local astrology groups and has taught at adult educational centers in the Washington, D.C. area. She has been interviewed on several radio shows and was videoed by MSN Money for their series, "Find Your Dream Job at 55."

In 2006, Dianne founded the Holistic Entrepreneurs Alliance, a business networking and support group with meetings in northern Virginia. She holds a Certificate in Association Management from the American Society of Association Executives. Dianne worked 35 years in the corporate world, including several years in executive positions within nonprofit organizations before establishing her full-time astrological consulting practice.

Dianne is available for private sessions and to speak to your organization. She can be contacted through her website: www. SpiritinMatters.com.

Breinigsville, PA USA
30 June 2010
240980BV00002B/2/P